IF I'M
HONEST

Tim Stafford
and
Philip Yancey

f r a m e w o r k s

FRAMEWORKS
38 De Montfort Street, Leicester LE1 7GP, England

Unless otherwise stated, Scripture quotations in
this publication are from the Holy Bible, New
International Version. Copyright © 1973, 1978,
1984 International Bible Society. Published in
Great Britain by Hodder and Stoughton Ltd.

First British edition 1990

This edition issued by special arrangement with
Zondervan Publishing House, Grand Rapids,
Michigan, USA. (Original title: *Unhappy secrets of
the Christian life*.)

British Library Cataloguing in Publication Data
Stafford, Tim
  If I'm honest.
  1. Unhappy secrets of the Christian life
  I. Title   II. Yancey, Philip
  248.4
ISBN 0–85111–213–7

Set in 10 on 12 Palatino
by Input Typesetting Ltd, London SW19 8DR
Printed in Great Britain by Cox & Wyman Ltd,
Reading

*Frameworks is an imprint of Inter-Varsity Press, the
book-publishing division of the Universities and
Colleges Christian Fellowship.*

CONTENTS

feelings don't always reflect reality. You can feel that God is far away, for instance, when in fact he is immediately available.

C H A P T E R

Sometimes, though, you feel far from God for what seems a very realistic reason. Do you know what I find more discouraging then anything else in my life as a Christian?

TEMPTATION:
Why do I give in?
Is it possible to stop?

It's the feeling I get right after I have given in, again, to temptation – after I look at a dirty magazine, for instance.

Temptation is so pervasive, so personal. Doesn't God understand that we humans cannot simply flip an internal switch and automatically say 'no' to everything? I find myself failing again and again and again.

So I have thought about temptation, wondering why God allows it, and whether there is a magic secret to resisting it. 'Yielding to God' or 'turning to the Lord' are phrases that have helped me at times. But I have found there is no magic in phrases. I cannot turn away from temptation just by putting myself through some mental gymnastics.

Such religious 'techniques' have sometimes left me very discouraged. They make me think I have the answer. Then, giving in to temptation again, I abruptly know that I don't. And my doubts return.

*t*aking a closer look

It has helped, though, to think through the nature of temptation. Is there some consistent trend I can discern in it? I have found three different components to temptation.

Temptation can be a physical object you encounter.
- A beautiful woman you can easily turn into an object instead of a person by letting her body preoccupy your thoughts.
- A piece of pie when you're on a diet.
- Too much change returned by a cashier.

If you want to avoid temptation, avoid these objects as much as you possibly can. Unfortunately, some are not easy to stay away from without becoming a hermit.

Temptation is a pressured situation.
- When everyone kids you and eggs you to do something you would rather not.
- When your boss jumps on your back, and you feel like lashing out at him or her.
- When you are in a group of strangers who

"Temptation is so pervasive, so personal."

"So many things that I know are wrong look so good . . . "

are laughing and having a good time among themselves, and you feel like creeping away and feeling sorry for yourself.

By yourself you might not want to do the things those situations tempt you to do. You wouldn't gossip if you weren't around friends who were gossiping. You wouldn't swear if your friends didn't. In certain situations, however, you find yourself doing what you otherwise would not.

Some of those situations you can stay away from, just as you can stay away from tempting objects. Other situations you may be able to defuse. One well-placed remark may loosen up a tense moment. You can become a leader in your group instead of a follower. You can sit down with your boss and explain how you feel so that he or she won't be so prone to jump on you.

Unfortunately, some pressured situations are not easy to avoid or change. Temptation seems inevitable.

Temptation is a voice in your head trying to deceive you.

- 'You're worthless. Why try?'
- 'If they treat you like that, you ought to treat them the same way. They deserve it.'
- 'What difference does it make if you do it one more time?'

Temptation works from inside, calling into question what God says is true and scattering half-truths inside your mind. This is the most devastating aspect of temptation. Tempting objects and pressuring situations are not enough. They must be accompanied by an invasion of your brain. Obviously you can't run from your own thoughts. You can be tempted anywhere, anytime – in church, alone, in the wilderness (where, in fact, Jesus was most severely tempted). So how are *you* going to 'avoid temptation'?

You can't, really. Some people try to lock temptation out of their lives. They go only to 'safe' parties and 'safe' films, and they have 'safe' friends. They build up a set of rules for themselves to follow rigidly so that temptation will never find a crack in their personalities. All these actions may be appropriate at times. But any real solution has to deal with the brain as well. If you are free from temptation in your own thoughts, you can conquer the problems friends and things bring into your life.

" . . . and sometimes I give in."

a helpful analogy

The pressure of temptation is a lot like real, physical pressure. You can 'escape' it only to a point. Do you think a submarine, since it's watertight, can go down as deep as it likes? It can't. Even the nuclear submarines, built strongly enough to batter through the ice at the North Pole, have a maximum depth. A submarine known as *Thresher* exceeded that depth some years ago. When the pressure became too great, the sea water crushed the sub's heavy steel bulkheads as if the submarine were a plastic model. Searchers found only little pieces of that huge ship lying on the ocean floor. That is pressure.

What if you want to go deeper than a submarine can go? There are research crafts built especially for that purpose – steel balls lowered in to the ocean on a cable. One

"Some Christians deal with pressure by putting on inches of steel plate."

researcher can just fit inside, shielded by the heavy steel armour. As he descends, he peers out through a thick glass plate, searching the ocean depths for whatever life may survive under such pressure.

And what does he see? Fish. You might expect these fish, living under such pressure, to be built along the lines of an army tank. They are not. Where the little submarine has inches of steel to protect it, these fish have normal skin, a fraction of an inch thick. They swim freely and curiously about the craft. They sometimes flash neon lights. They are as exotic as any fish in the ocean.

How can they survive so freely under such pressure? They have a secret: equal and opposite pressure inside themselves.

In real life, some Christians deal with pressure by putting on inches of steel plate. They shield themselves from the outside world and strap themselves into a narrow space, peering out into the darkness. They are safe inside. But God's kind of freedom is more like the fish's. We keep our shape, not through steel plate, but by God's Spirit, who gives us inside strength to deal with each pressure point in our lives.

Romans 12:2, a noted Bible passage, essentially says: 'Don't be squeezed into the mould of this world, but be transformed by the renewing of your mind.' Pressure from the outside acts to make you conform – to be just like everyone else. The Spirit of God counteracts that from the inside, through your mind.

It's no use pretending temptation doesn't exist. If you are on a diet, a piece of pie looks appealing, and there's nothing evil about that. I have heard people say that sin is really no fun, but that is not true. Sin *is* fun . . . for a while.

What makes sin not fun in the long run are the things that come with it. You may enjoy a piece of pie today, but that means tomorrow you won't enjoy standing on the scales. You may enjoy self-pity today, but if you keep it up, self-pity will become *all* you get to enjoy: you won't have any friends.

*b*eating temptation

To change your mind to have the inner strength to push back temptation, you need to appeal to higher loyalties, stronger desires. If you think of it, resisting temptation is basically simple. It's a choice. You can look over the options and decide what you want to do. The problem is that temptation's pleasures are often more obvious and immediate than the pleasures of not giving in. Besides, your mind has been twisted so you cannot always see clearly what is really good for you. It *does* seem better to be loved by your crowd of friends than to be loved by God. So you need to renew your mind – get in touch with what's really best for you. You need to retrain your thinking so that those rewards become as obvious as the rewards you get for giving in to temptation. Perhaps these principles will help that process.

" . . . these principles will help . . . "

Know what you're getting into. Think about the long-term results of how you act. Today it may be easier to fight with your parents and get your own way. But what kind of relationship are you building for the future? On the other hand, what will obeying God lead to? If you can see the attraction of the life God wants for you, you will be less tempted to choose some other, short-term pleasure.

The Bible is full of commentary on how good a godly life is. Many of the psalms speak of the sheer enjoyment of being in touch with God, obedient to him, relishing the joys of his world. Some of the psalms also frankly confront the doubts and bitter feelings that come when you see unbelievers happy and successful without God, while your godliness seems unrewarded. Read those psalms and work on appreciating the advantages of not giving in to temptation. Do it daily.

(for instance, Psalms 37, 49, 73)

Replace tempting thoughts with something better. You can't ignore temptation, but you can fill your thoughts with other things. Often prayer helps – and not necessarily prayer for help in resisting temptation. I often begin praying for friends. Sometimes, too, when you are feeling tempted it is very helpful to remind yourself of the power and love of Jesus, who is on your side, who lives with you. Some people use this verse 'I can do everything through him [Christ] who gives me strength.'

(Philippians 4:13)

You don't have to fill your mind with religious thoughts. Sometimes the best thing you can do is to pick up an interesting book, call up a friend, or start working on a project. If you are tempted to go to an X-rated movie, look for another movie instead. The problem with many temptations is that they are close and immediate. If you can put them off a while and give your mind a chance to recover from its panic, you will be in better shape to see the bigger picture.

Your mind tends to follow patterns. Change patterns, and you change your mind. In some families, kids are always fighting over what TV programmes to watch. They should change the pattern by figuring out ahead of time what shows they will watch and reach some compromise long before the tube is turned on.

For me, being tired often means getting depressed. I can lecture myself that I have no right to feel so sorry for myself. But a more effective solution is to go to bed when I am tired. Somehow that takes the drama out of resisting temptation. I outflank it instead of pacing the floor and praying for strength to resist it.

Breaking habits often requires persistent hard work. You must first find out what starts you into the pattern leading to failure. Then, you must break the pattern in its beginning stages. No matter how innocent those early stages may seem, you must be merciless with them. People seldom break a bad pattern overnight. Gradually, painfully, they fight their way out of it.

Break the pattern of failure by confession. When you go over your mistakes with another person, it changes your attitude. For one thing, you receive forgiveness, and your mind is put at rest. You don't get down on yourself and repeat your failures because of an 'I-did-it-once-what-does-one-more-time-matter?' attitude. For another thing, a friend can help strengthen you. He or she can check up on you, encourage you, and pray for you. He or she can remind you of God's limitless forgiveness.

"You can't ignore temptation . . ."

" . . . everyone has at least one area of special weakness."

11

God's limitless forgiveness

As you try to identify and break bad patterns, remember that everyone has at least one area of special weakness. There you may find temptation too strong. You may become discouraged and doubtful of God's goodness.

At these times you must remember the limitless nature of God's forgiveness. It *is* limitless, which is hard for us to grasp. But if you cling to it, you will be lifted out of your discouragement. Not only that, but the area you are weakest in can be transformed into a special strength.

Above all, remember who you are: A child of God, loved by him. When tempting thoughts come, say to yourself: 'I could act that way, but does that really bring honour to God? Because of the way he treats me, I want to be loyal and loving to him.'

The more you understand God's love, the more you will want to be close to him and obedient to him. As you grow in Christ, some of your temptations will simply vanish – they will begin to seem stupid. Their pleasures will be insignificant compared with the good things you are experiencing.

Many people have found that studying Scripture, and even memorizing certain verses, can help in resisting temptation. Not that it's magic, quoting Scripture to make the problems go away. It simply reminds you of the voice of God himself and of his desires for your life. Jesus, when tempted by Satan, referred back to the book of Deuteronomy and found his guidance there. You can too –

so long as you know Scripture well enough to be able to use it under pressure.

Reinforce your understanding of your true identity not only by reading the Bible and applying what it says, but also by talking to God, by talking with Christian friends, by listening to what pastors and other Christians say, and especially by worshipping and thanking God for what he has done for you. The disciplined habit of going to church and having fellowship with other Christians is a powerful force in shaping your sense of being in Christ's family. Christ's message to you is this: you simply don't have to act in the old way. You are a new person with a whole new way of acting. Jesus will help you live up to your new self.

"You simply don't have to act in the old way."

You get stronger every time you beat temptation. Each success is an exercise building you up. Perhaps that's part of the reason God permits temptation rather than taking it all away: because it gives you a chance to strengthen your spiritual muscles, to focus on the things in life that are most important. When you're under temptation, you can have no doubt about needing God's help. When you resist temptation through God's help, you have no doubt about the direction you have chosen: it's wonderful to work on God's side.

There will always be temptations as long as you live on this earth. And you will always fail God at some point. Both temptation and failure should remind you to rely on God for forgiveness of your sins, for the desire to change your life, and the power to change your life. The closer you come to God, the less you will want to disappoint him. And the less you will doubt his purposes for you.

T. S.

13

kathy grew up in a church where she got the idea that God watched her like a hawk from heaven, counting up her

sins. You could see by the way she walked and the way her eyes never met anyone else's that she was ashamed to be alive.

Eventually, she came to

GUILT:
If I'm forgiven, why do I feel so guilty?

understand that Jesus was willing to take her just the way she was, to love her and heal her from all guiltiness. For a while she walked around feeling as though she had new running shoes: everything seemed lighter, happier, and freer.

Strangely, this sensation wore off. Her initial wonder at being accepted and loved grew old. Many of the patterns she had expected God to change hung on. She still did things she knew God didn't like, and she began feeling guilty again.

It did not help that Kathy went to a church where guilt was regularly hammered in. When she read a chapter of the Bible that others found encouraging, she found every word aimed at her failures. A single word about sin was enough to bring a week-long attack of guilt. She was just naturally sensitive, and after the initial relief of forgiveness had worn off, her Christianity seemed to make her guilt greater not less.

A non-Christian psychologist, concluding that most of her problems were related to her faith, tried to 'cure' her of that. He did not believe in such a thing as guilt. He thought the best thing for everyone was to 'feel good about yourself'. For Kathy, he certainly had a point: guilt paralysed her. It kept her from serving others. She even began to question whether she really was a Christian.

It was difficult to argue with Kathy about her guilt. To her Christian friends, the sins bothering her didn't seem very great. They certainly had greater problems which didn't paralyse them with guilt. In fact, when they talked to her they felt uncomfortable: maybe they should feel as guilty as she did! They didn't know how to help Kathy. They could only listen to her while she spilled out her guilty feelings.

"You could see . . . she was ashamed to be alive."

an unreliable conscience

Kathy was an extreme case, but by no means a unique one. Many psychologists would list guilt as one of the chief problems of their disturbed clients. Often it seems to afflict the most religious people. Why does Christianity, which promises to forgive and heal guilt, sometimes seem to bring on more?

The instrument that tells you that you're guilty is usually called the conscience. It communicates through your emotions and warns you when there is a problem in your life.

The conscience is very much like your body's pain-sensing system. When you cut your finger, the dripping blood is an indisputable fact. Anyone can see that it needs attention. But the pain that comes with the cut makes it urgent. This can be very annoying if you are doing something you want to do, like learning a new move on your skateboard or climbing a rock face. You would rather put off dealing with your cut. But pain won't let you.

Your conscience is designed to respond in the same way to sin. If something is wrong in your life, guilty feelings force your attention onto the sore spot, making you drop everything else until you attend to it. It is God's way of making you feel the same way he feels about sin. But one huge problem comes up: your conscience is unreliable. Sometimes it sends guilt messages which are inaccurate or inappropriate.

Your pain-sensing system is, by contrast, quite reliable. If you feel physical pain there is nearly always a cut to go with it. Yet imaginary pains do exist. Amputees sometimes receive terrible pain from a 'phantom limb' that no longer exists.

Such imaginary problems show up much more often with your conscience. One person feels guilty from premarital sex, and

" . . . I worry . . . because I can't keep in line and do his will."

another doesn't. One person feels guilty because he stole from Sainsbury's, and another doesn't. One person feels guilty for going to a dance, while another wouldn't even think about it. The explanation is simple: God made your pain-sensing system, but your conscience is largely man-made. We tend to think that our conscience is the voice of God, but it is really more the voice of our parents and our society, plus our experience, formed over many years. If you were brought up well, your conscience will usually be fairly accurate. If you were brought up poorly, or spent years turning off your conscience's warnings, your conscience may be far out of register.

In other words, real guilt is not the same as guilt feelings. People like Kathy are mostly plagued with false, not real, guilt. They have an oversensitive conscience which isn't tuned in to the reality of God's teaching in the Bible. Someone needs to ask Kathy, 'Is this real guilt or false?' Often people who have a bad self-image use false or imagined guilt to punish themselves.

*d*istinguishing false guilt from true

A sign of false guilt is that you can't pin it down. False guilt often arises in response to persistent mental fantasies, to feelings and temptations. It seldom stems from a specific action that can be changed. If it does, the action is frequently morally arguable – such as masturbation or dancing – or something done long in the past. I have noticed that chronically guilty people seldom agonize over something the Bible indisputably condemns. They worry about the grey areas.

This leads me to think that false guilt is often a temptation sent by Satan, meant to divert our attention from God's wonderful forgiveness and from real problems that God wants to change. False guilt needs to be faced for exactly what it is. If you experience false guilt, don't pray to God (for the hundredth time) to forgive it. Instead, ask him to help you leave such self-hating feelings behind and get on with life.

In fact, this is just what 1 John 3:18–20 suggests:

Our love should not be just words and talk; it must be true love, which shows itself in action. This, then, is how we will know that we belong to the truth. This is how our hearts will be confident in God's presence. If our heart condemns us, we know that God is greater than our heart, and that he knows everything.

(1 John 3:18–20, GNB)

Rather than being paralysed by guilt, we are to get on with obeying God through active love. Nothing can better reassure us of God's real love.

You can tune your conscience to reality – though it takes time – by confronting false guilt, and by trying to absorb God's biblical standards of right and wrong. A bad conscience is man-made – and so is a good one. If you surround yourself with people who reinforce God's standards and challenge your 'false guilt', you will gradually begin to think as they do.

" . . . paralysed by guilt . . . "

A good, accurate conscience is basically a short-cut. It helps you know what you ought to do without having to ponder your action. In a sense a conscience is an automatic pilot. Your conscience will guide you through millions of choices each day without a thought. You don't have to think about whether to pay for the shirt you pick up at a department store. You don't have to ponder whether to accept what your father said about getting in on time. You don't have to wonder whether to cheat each time you take a test. Your conscience saves you the trouble. It lets you concentrate on more difficult choices.

But your conscience is not an infallible guide. It is not the voice of God. It is an emotional response that God has built into your brain. It can be, if you tune it properly, a helpful instrument pushing you to do the right thing. Left untuned, however, it can paralyse you or distract you from what is really important in God's sight.

" . . . false guilt."

When you're really guilty

So far we have been considering what I call false guilt. What if your guilt is real? What do you do then? I can think of three possible responses.

One is to *punish yourself*. 'I must be a terrible person. Oh, how guilty I am! How much God must feel hurt by me!' This is like a person who, on cutting his finger, sits down in the road and begins to yowl, endlessly screaming how much it hurts. Little children do this, but adults should not. It is not a very good way to respond to pain – or to guilt feelings.

Another response is to *deny that the guilt*

19

exists at all. 'Guilt is a neurotic impulse. It cripples and represses many wonderful people and keeps them from enjoying life. God wants me to feel happy. Therefore I will never let myself feel guilty.' This is like a person who makes up his mind to totally ignore pain: 'Pain is a weakness. Only weak people feel pain. I'm tough, too tough for that.' The macho act of ignoring pain turns you into a totally insensitive person. Ignoring guilt will also make you insensitive, and you will usually end up inflicting much more real guilt on yourself, whether you feel that guilt or not. In our time, when the only duty a person is supposed to have is to 'feel good about himself', a lot of real guilt gets denied.

"I had no good reason for my grudge . . ."

A third response is to *try to find out* what is making you feel guilty and stop it. By analogy, this is like feeling a sharp pain in your foot, and taking your shoe off to find the source. That is the right way to deal with pain. In fact, the whole point of pain is to grab your attention. Similarly, guilt feelings are meant to make you find the source of your feelings.

As a student in college I went through one of the worst depressions of my life. After a few days of real blackness, when I repeatedly cried out to God for help and seemed to get no answer, the idea occurred to me that I might be doing something wrong. Was there anything in my life that I knew quite well was sinful?

There was, as it turned out. I had been resenting a pastor of a nearby church. I had no good reason for my grudge: I just didn't like his style.

I certainly could not see any connection

between that grudge and the depression I was in. But I decided that I would try to do something about it. That week I went, somewhat painfully, to a Bible study the pastor was conducting. I decided I would keep going, whether I wanted to or not, and learn to love that man. My depression vanished. As the weeks went on, I gained a great deal of insight from the Bible study. I believe that at least part of my depression was caused by guilt – the guilt of holding a grudge, of cutting myself off from another Christian.

I do not mean, by this, to start anyone on a fit of introspection. That is not healthy. We can all find plenty of sins if we are willing to look hard enough, and some of us even invent sins that aren't there at all. Don't do that. Just ask: Does God want me to do something that I have been ignoring? Is it clearly something God wants for me, something that other Christians would agree on? If so, do it. Don't pray long, weepy prayers for forgiveness. Just change your behaviour.

" . . . I just didn't like his style."

*h*ealing the wounds

But you also need healing. When you have fallen down, you can make a decision not to run so carelessly any more, but you still have a scraped knee that needs healing medicine. Guilt also needs medicine: the medicine of God's forgiveness and care. Once again, 1 John helps: 'If we confess our sins, he is faithful and just and will forgive us our sins and purify us from all unrighteousness.'

(1 John 1:9)

Let us not make this a big, soul-searching

issue. It is as simple as it sounds. The only requirement is that your confession be sincere: 'God, I realize that I was wrong and you were right. I messed it up, and I'm sorry. Will you forgive me and set me on the right track again?' That is *all* it takes, and John makes it clear that after such an action God will cleanse you from *all* your sinfulness. God doesn't clean you up 80% or begin a long process that may take years. There, on the spot, he cleanses you.

I find an interesting discrepancy between the way most religious people deal with guilt and the way the Bible deals with it. We are preoccupied with all the shades of guilt. Preachers sometimes urge us to search for it in our hearts. We are to find it, confess it, and then go on to find more. Some people, poor souls, are tortured with a lot of guilt; other people, lucky ones, feel very little guilt. If only the former could become more like the latter. Good news, we say. They can! If they work at it long enough they can produce a positive self-image, a deep emotional security in the fact that God loves them. Of course, they can also become better people, with less to feel guilty about!

The Bible draws a different, bigger picture. There you find no question of adding up columns of guilt to see how much progress you have made. It is plain: everyone has sinned and has fallen short of what God wants him or her to be. Then forgiveness comes with a bang. You were 100% guilty, and suddenly you are 100% not guilty. Full and utter forgiveness is free to anyone who wants it.

I think it is important to keep this big picture brilliant in our minds. The small picture

" 'What if I don't go to heaven with everyone else I know?' "

is our slow, individual advances. The big picture is the explosive advance that God offers us all in his Son, Jesus Christ. Someone like Kathy needs to be told this again and again until it gets through.

An old story captures this message better than anything I know. It tells about a man who has been involved in some sinful pattern for longer than he cares to think about. How many times has he confessed this miserable sin to God, promising that he will never do it again? And now he comes to God again, confessing the same thing: 'Lord, I could die with shame. Again and again I have done this thing. I confess it to you, and promise that I will never, ever sin this way again. Will you forgive me?' From heaven come the words, 'I forgive you. It is all forgotten. You are clean to start over again.'

So the man feels wonderfully free. God has forgiven him. What more can he ask? All afternoon he revels in the belief that he will never fall into that same sin again. And then, that very night, temptation comes to him and he fails.

He can hardly bring himself to pray. Wasn't it just this morning he fervently promised God he would never sin that way again? He almost makes up his mind to ignore it, and maybe God won't notice. But his guilty conscience gets to him, and finally he begins to talk to God.

'God, I'm so embarrassed I can hardly talk to you. I did it again.'

'Did what?'

'That sin. The one we talked about just this morning.'

'I don't remember any sin.'

T. S.

Christians believe that the Bible is the best book that was ever written — a gift to us from God himself. The Bible doesn't merely

tell us about God, it is a channel for him to come directly to us. Through reading the Bible we can meet with God and hear his voice speaking to us.

THE BIBLE:
Why can't I read God's Word?

This belief, while well-founded, sets people up for some unsettling surprises. A Gallup Poll revealed that the majority of Americans believe the Bible to be divinely inspired. Yet only a small percentage of those same Americans could name four of the Ten Commandments or other equally basic Bible facts. For the majority, the Bible sits somewhere on a shelf, impressive to look at, but unread.

Even committed Christians fail. In a survey

initiated by *Campus Life* magazine, young
Christians repeatedly mentioned their guilt
for not reading the Bible consistently. They
believed in the Bible. They expected to find
help there. They saw it as a holy book. But
they did not read the Bible nearly so often as
they thought they should, and this frustrat-
ing paradox was a major reason for them to
doubt their faith.

After all, if God really wants to speak to
you, and makes himself available to you
every day, and yet you never 'find time' to
listen to his voice – what kind of Christian are
you?

*" . . . the Bible
seemed as
appetizing as
yesterday's
coffee."*

Secrets about the Bible

Should this paradox cause people to doubt
their faith? I don't think so. The paradox
doesn't usually come from a lack of real
belief. It comes, I think, from some un-
realistic expectations about the Bible.

In most churches, people talk about the
great benefits of reading the Bible. They
don't say much about how hard that reading
can be. People openly tell about the times
when the Bible encouraged, corrected, or
inspired them. They keep secret the times
when the Bible seemed as appetizing as yesterday's coffee.

I'm quite sure that most Christians struggle
all through their lives to read and understand
the Bible. Few if any find it enjoyable all the
time. They rarely mention this, especially to
younger Christians, for fear it would discour-
age them. Actually, by keeping the difficulty
of the Bible a secret they increase others'

"Why does it have to be so hard to understand?"

guilty frustration. Young Christians especially think there must be something wrong with them if they don't find the Bible a consistent inspiration.

For several years I have been involved with a project meant to overcome barriers to Bible reading. (The result of our work: the NIV Student Bible.) We used modern research techniques to try to find an answer to the question. 'What keeps you from reading the Bible?' The encouraging news was that the vast majority of young Christians had a very high view of the Scripture. They expected good things from the Bible. The discouraging news was that very few of them found those good things on a consistent basis. Only a small percentage of them could claim they read the Bible on anything close to a regular basis. When asked why, they gave answers that fell ino three categories: 'I get discouraged', 'I can't understand it', 'I can't find anything.'

'I get discouraged.' Simple discouragement is by far the most common reason for not reading the Bible. Most of the people in our research felt guilty: every experiment they had tried in Bible reading had ended in failure.

The Bible is a big book, over one thousand pages long. How many people have read any other one-thousand-page book? People who start with Genesis, planning to read through the whole Bible, very often get bogged down somewhere around Numbers or Deuteronomy. Fatigue sets in. I would guess that about the same number who complete *War and Peace* also finish the Bible.

A great many more people never even start. Their busy schedules and their limited confidence keep them from starting a project they feel sure they'll fail to complete. Instead, they read occasionally from familiar passages like Philippians or the Psalms. But to venture out into unfamiliar books – they wouldn't know where to begin.

'I can't understand it.' Lack of basic understanding creates a second, major barrier to Bible reading. Today many readers have grown up with very little exposure to the Bible. They may never have heard of Goliath or Abraham. Often they ask, 'What is the point of reading about spears and chariots and village wells and leprosy?'

Because it was written several thousand years ago, the Bible presents a culture gap: it uses hard-to-pronounce names and refers to many outdated customs. For most readers, the Bible is the most ancient book in their library. They find it hard and confusing to read Shakespeare – and Shakespeare is only a fraction as old as the Bible.

'I can't find anything.' 'I spend so much time just flipping through the Bible looking for something,' many people say. Bible readers are often looking for help on specific issues – but they don't know where to find it. Everybody has heard of something from the Bible: the Ten Commandments, the Golden Rule, the story of Daniel in the lions' den. But how do you know where to look for them? The Bible is too large just to flip through on a random search.

Until you have run into these three

problems, you really don't know much about the Bible. The Bible is not an easy read. But who said it should be?

Because the Bible is a holy book, a gift from God, we sometimes act as though it is not a book at all. It becomes a magical symbol: a black cover or gilt edges set it apart. In reality, the Bible's holiness doesn't come from its appearance. It comes from its ability to communicate the Word of God to us. It does this in much the same way that other books do: we have to read and understand. I don't have anything against black covers or gilt edges. But I do object to the misconceptions that damage Christians' ability to read and understand.

misconceptions

1: The Bible is an inspirational book. The Bible is inspiring, of course. 'Inspire' comes from a Latin word meaning 'to breathe'. The Bible inspires by breathing new life into us, the life of the Holy Spirit of God. But how does the Bible do it? Not in the way that 'inspirational' books do.

'Inspirational' books are usually full of poetic encouragement. They make you feel great. They bring a catch to your throat and tears to your eyes. Usually you can pick up an inspirational book at any point, read a page or two, and find yourself emotionally moved. The Bible is not inspirational in this sense. Oh, it is in places. But a great deal of it isn't. Most of it isn't pitched at your emotions at all, but at your mind. The Bible 'inspires' primarily by reforming and teaching. Some

" . . . the Bible . . . becomes a magical symbol . . . "

of that is downright unpleasant, especially where it tells you what you are doing wrong and warns you of the consequences.

If you do go to the Bible thinking it is 'inspirational reading', you will often be disappointed, and you will eventually restrict your reading to just a few small parts of the Bible, such as the Psalms (though not all the psalms, either – some are far from 'inspirational'). On the other hand, if you go to the Bible expecting to learn what God is doing in the world and what he expects of you, you will be inspired. You will learn what God is like, and that will breathe 'new life' into you.

"It's not a religious version of a dictionary of quotations . . ."

2: The Bible is a collection of wonderful verses. I think this misconception comes partly from the way the Bible is used in sermons. Many pastors, knowing the Bible well, quote from a variety of verses scattered through the Bible. Each one of these is a gem. Some Bibles also list verses you can look at for help in times of trouble, discouragement, temptation, and other trials.

Unfortunately, some people get the idea that the Bible is a treasury of great and inspiring fragments. Unfortunately, though they hunt for them, they rarely find them. The Bible is not a religious version of a dictionary of quotations, providing raw material for greetings cards and car stickers. It happens to have some great quotes in it, but if you read the book just to find the great quotes, you will miss the author's point.

To understand God's Word, you need to read it paragraph by paragraph, chapter by chapter, book by book. You need to get a sense of the whole story. This means that you have to read long passages. You can't just look for a 'thought for the day'. But why should we expect any different? Our God is a big God. He has a big story to tell. You can't fit him on a windscreen sticker.

3: You don't need any help to understand the Bible. This idea probably developed out of the Reformation, which rebelled – rightly, I think – against church leaders suggesting that ordinary people couldn't read the Bible and understand God's message for themselves. God's Word speaks to people at many levels of sophistication, and often a very uneducated person can teach someone with a Ph.D. Listening to God's voice doesn't require a graduate degree.

But this fact seems to encourage some people to think that ideally you should take the Bible into the privacy of your room, open it up, and let God speak to you in a way that he speaks to no-one else. In a mysterious way, you will be given unexplainable secrets of understanding.

God's Spirit does have some personal messages for you. But the more clearly you understand the Bible, the more clearly the Spirit can speak through it. You understand the Bible just as you understand most books – first by reading it, then by discussing it with others, and finally by being taught about it by people who have studied the book much longer than you have. This is particularly true of an ancient book dealing with unfamiliar customs and geography.

Most people who successfully read the Bible get help. A lot of them are in a Bible study group. Many use Bible study guides, commentaries, Bible dictionaries, or have Bibles with explanatory notes. These aids do not interfere with the process by which God's Spirit speaks to us. They assist.

*P*ractical solutions

The Bible is a book to be mastered. It requires the full commitment of your whole self: body, mind, and spirit. Your body comes into it as you discipline yourself to sit still and read, just as you discipline yourself to do your homework. Your mind comes into it as you grapple to understand, just as you grapple with mathematics or any other difficult subject. Your spirit comes into it as you submit to the truth as God gives it. God calls all of you, and responding to his call is a life-long challenge.

Yet it is utterly unlike mathematics homework. Does reading the Bible sound grim? It isn't. As you respond to God, he breathes new life into you. Increasingly, you want to do what he says. Increasingly, you love his Word – the actual words in the Bible, as well as the way God uses them in your life. Talk to someone who's run a marathon or climbed a mountain and you'll get the idea. They may say it was the hardest thing they ever did. But the pride in achievement and the sense of being changed for ever by the experience override the difficulty.

Practically speaking, you need help if you are to succeed at reading the Bible. It's like training for a marathon: only you can do it, but some ways are easier than others.

First of all, you need a Bible in a modern

" . . . the sense of being changed for ever . . . "

" . . . God doesn't command you to have a 'quiet time'."

translation. Lots of people have the idea that the Bible sounds 'more like the Bible' in the King James Version. The King James is a great translation, but it is as ancient as Shakespeare. Most people can't understand it easily. The Bible really sounds 'more like the Bible' when you read and understand it – not when you like the way the words vibrate against your eardrums. Many newer translations are at least as accurate as the King James, and they are far easier to understand.

Second, you need a realistic system for reading the Bible. Don't start at Genesis and try to work your way through. Don't aimlessly flip through the Bible looking for 'good stuff'. Start with two or three of the basic books in the New Testament, such as Luke (an account of Jesus' life) and Ephesians. When you've read and understood them pretty well, ask a pastor or someone you trust to recommend what to read next.

A number of excellent systems for reading the whole Bible exist. Unfortunately, most of them ask you to read several chapters a day, and they concentrate on getting through the whole Bible. A beginning Bible reader should probably not try to read much more than one chapter a day, and he or she should concentrate on some of the books in the Bible that are easiest to understand. Later on, you can go on to do more.

Third, you need to develop a consistent time when you read the Bible each day. This isn't a moral issue – God doesn't command you to have a 'quiet time'. It's a practical issue. The Bible is such a long book that only regular reading, year after year, will enable you to know it well. Daily reading helps you take its wisdom into daily life. Bit by bit, God's Word becomes part of your thinking. Very few people spontaneously read the Bible every day. Most people must make it a habit at a particular time, day in, day out.

Fourth, you should seek out other Christians who can help you understand the Bible. Many churches and Christian organizations have Bible study programmes where small groups of people study the Bible together. These can help tremendously, especially where a well-trained leader leads the group.

Fifth, it is a good idea to spend some money for materials to help you understand the Bible. A Christian bookshop can provide you with many options:

- *Bible study guides* take you through certain books of the Bible, or through certain themes. You can hardly work your way through one of these fill-in-the-blank booklets without learning something.
- *Study Bibles* contain footnotes and other explanatory notes. When you buy a study Bible, don't be impressed by the sheer volume and complexity of the notes. Read some of the explanations and make sure that you will really understand them. It's better to buy a simple one you will really use than an impressive one that confuses you.
- *Commentaries* are books that explain and comment on the Bible, usually verse by verse. You can buy one for the whole Bible, or, more commonly, one for a particular book of the Bible. Commentaries vary tremendously. Ask someone you trust for recommendations.
- *A Bible dictionary* is really more of an encyclopaedia (in one volume) than a dictionary. Any

subject you are interested in – 'David', 'faith', 'prophecy' – will get a brief but thorough explanation. All the places, people, and books of the Bible get covered.

● *A concordance* tells you where to find all the verses that use a particular word. If you're interested in 'faith', all the times the Bible uses that word will be listed. A concordance is particularly useful if you want to study a subject in depth.

You don't need all of these helps. You don't necessarily need any of them. But they can help in a difficult task.

*t*he disturbing word 'difficult'

Difficult? Lots of people feel disturbed by that word 'difficult'. It makes reading the Bible sound as attractive as writing an exam paper. Many people want reading the Bible to be as relaxing as a warm bath. It isn't. Parts of it are. Overall, it's more like training for sports. It feels great when you do it. But it is hard work.

Consider the alternatives. You can hold on to your misconceptions about what the Bible should be like – and you can keep right on feeling guilty, and short of the breath of God.

Or you can accept the Bible for what it is – a long, challenging book that requires all you have, during all your life. If you accept this challenge, you can approach it intelligently, with commitment, and succeed. God will speak to you through his Word, and the speech will grow clearer and clearer.

T. S.

i shall call him Mr Thomas. He seldom missed church. He always prayed longer than anyone else and was most concerned about

4

the 'spiritual' dimensions of any problem. Yet he had cheated his relatives out of the family business, was a snoop, a liar, and, to top it all off, overweight.

HYPOCRITES:
If Christ is real, why does his church have so many phonies?

Though I haven't seen him in years, I would still find it hard to enjoy shaking hands with him. He exuded slime. When I hear the word hypocrite *I think of him.*

Phoney excuses

Hypocrites are an easy excuse. Ask someone why he or she doesn't go to church, for instance, and you are likely to hear, 'Because the church is full of hypocrites.'

That answer helps him or her avoid saying, 'Because I don't want to get up on Sunday mornings' or 'Because I don't believe in God the way Christians do' or 'Because I like my life the way it is and don't want to get close to something that might make me change.' These, and plenty others, would be honest reasons.

But someone who says the church is full of hypocrites puts the questioner on the defensive and doesn't have to deal with the real issues. That is why I have heard this excuse so often. I have also heard many Christians hedge defensively when somebody offers it.

"He exuded slime."

I overheard a non-Christian friend try a variation of it. When asked why he wasn't a Christian, he explained that he had been raised a Catholic. He described several things wrong with the nuns he had encountered: their uptightness, their severity, their mumbo-jumbo religion. He was hung up with those nuns; that was why, he said, he wasn't a Christian.

The person asking the question then broke into a laugh. 'You mean,' he asked incredulously, 'that you're going to let a few little ladies in uniforms keep you from knowing God?' Since then I have had an answer when someone tells me hypocrites keep him from becoming a Christian. 'Are you trying to say that a few hypocrites are enough to keep you from meeting God personally?'

That helps deal with the excuse, leaving you free to talk about genuine issues. But aren't there times when hypocrites are a genuine issue? For most people they are just an excuse, but are they always? Even as a

Christian I am bothered by the existence of hypocrites – people like Mr Thomas. They raise troublesome questions. If Christianity is so wonderful, why aren't Christians more wonderful people?

Why is it you find liars in the same building where truth is exalted week after week? Why does the religion that changes lives have phonies everywhere? It's as shocking as going into a political party's headquarters and finding that the workers plan to vote against their leader. The insincerity surrounding the leader makes you doubt the person's credibility.

It is the real question, not the excuse, that I want to deal with here. Why are there hypocritical Christians, and what are we supposed to do with them?

"Why are there hypocritical Christians?"

behind the counterfeit

A hypocrite might be called a counterfeit Christian, and that term sheds light. Why do people counterfeit something? Only because that something is valuable. No-one counterfeits a parking ticket. No-one fakes a bad school report. Only more valuable objects are counterfeited: things like twenty-dollar bills, or fifty-pound notes.

People will pretend to be rich. They will fake being university professors or football players. They will not usually pretend to be child-beaters.

Why do people often pretend to know God intimately? Because knowing God is such a valuable thing they want people to think they do. In a way, the presence of hypocrites demonstrates how desirable real Christianity is.

A generation or two ago, people would join the church because that was what all decent people did. Today, you don't lose respect if you don't go to church or claim to be a Christian. The only reason to be a hypocritical Christian is that you think knowing God is valuable. I do not mean that hypocrites consciously calculate how to 'counterfeit' Christianity.

What is a hypocrite? Hypocrites are those trying to gain respect from every group they're in. Around Christians they act spiritual, because that is what they think will make them admired. Around other circles they act unspiritual, because that will win them another kind of admiration or power. They are chameleons, coloured by their environment. Not having enough character to be themselves, they are forced to try to live up to a set of contradictory standards.

Of course, they gain only misery. They don't fool many people for long. Christians are not the only ones disgusted by a hypocrite; even those who live unspiritually all the time look down on someone who tries to have it both ways.

So when I recognize a hypocrite, I have learned that the proper attitude is sadness. I am seeing a person who doesn't know who he or she really is. He or she is too weak to be consistent, and is probably miserable.

Yet it is one thing to know sadness is the proper attitude, and another to use it with love. I think of Mr Thomas again. I have a hard enough time loving family and friends. How am I to love this man, who is so false?

The only way is to see deeper into him: to

see the misery in his soul, and also to see somehow the real person buried under piles of lies and fears. Somewhere inside must be the person God made.

But how can I ignore all the obvious faults in a Mr Thomas? How can I discover the person God meant him to be if he can't discover it himself? I find that I understand someone like him only when I examine my own life carefully. When I look deeply into my own soul I discover that I am not much better than Mr Thomas.

"How am I to love this man, who is so false?"

*i*t's all in the attitude

Hypocrites say they believe one thing but live another. By that standard I am a hypocrite, and so are you. In fact, everyone who claims to be a Christian is in one sense a hypocrite. Did not Jesus tell us, 'You shall love the Lord your God with all your mind, soul and strength, and your neighbour as yourself'? And don't we agree that those words are the standard for life? But none of us lives up to them. The greatest difference between me and Mr Thomas is not whether I live up to my beliefs; on that score I am a failure too. The difference is in our attitude towards that failure.

(Luke 10:27)

Jesus once told a story about two men who prayed. The first man, a hypocritical religious leader, thanked God for his moral character, which was well above the norm. The other man, a notorious crook, was so ashamed of himself he could barely speak to God. He did not thank God for anything. All he asked for was mercy. Jesus commented that the second man, not the first, was pleasing to God.

(Luke 18:10)

39

"A lot of Christians talk real holy . . . "

The man was pleasing not because he had sinned less, but because of his humble attitude. He knew his faults, and he didn't try to hide them.

Now, which of those two men do you think might have been cynical about a church where he could find hypocrites? The first man, obviously. He would not think of himself as a hypocrite – he lived a good life and was proud of it. He looked down on those who abused the Ten Commandments. He would consider himself too good to attend a church of hypocrites.

You can't imagine that attitude in the second man. He was so aware of his own faults that it never occurred to him to be offended by other people's. It is this attitude that pleases God, Jesus says.

When I hear that story, I try to place myself in it. When I am upset about hypocrites, am I not like the first man? But when I look deep into myself and see how far my own hypocrisy goes, I become more like the second. Then, I don't have the courage (or the desire) to sneer at others – even at Mr Thomas.

Each of us comes to Jesus as a starving person after bread. What does it say about me if I turn around to sneer at other starving people who don't yet know where the bread is?

*b*ut . . . in church?

Of course, one big obstacle to accepting hypocrites is that we find them in church. If I meet someone who is dishonest and mean in the grocery store I am not going to spit on him or her. But aren't Christians supposed to be different? Doesn't the Bible call Christians holy people? If so, why do churches tolerate hypocrites?

The answer is that most churches try not to. They say loud and clear, almost every week, that dishonesty and selfishness keep us from really living. They encourage people to confront what is wrong with their lives. Some churches will take the extreme measure of expelling someone who consistently, outwardly sins and won't admit it and change.

It is difficult to see what more a church could do. Is there a hypocrisy test we could give everyone? That begins to sound like the Inquisition. Frankly, I wouldn't want anybody else testing *my* hypocrisy. And I don't feel competent to judge anyone else's. Who really knows another person's heart? How can we tell what a person thinks when he or she's alone? We can evaluate what someone does, but how can we evaluate his or her sincerity? I would much rather leave that sort of judging to God. If I understand the Bible correctly, some of his judgments will turn out to be surprising to us.

" . . . but then they gossip about someone . . . "

Beyond that, I have to ask what a church is supposed to be. Are we to separate out the pure people and pack them into a building once a week? Or are we to have open doors to those who are inconsisent and troubled?

The Bible calls Christians holy, but is that because they have resolved all hypocrisy and inconsistency in their lives? Not in my case. My only claim to 'holiness' is that, time and time again, I bring my hypocrisies and inconsistencies to Jesus and allow him to forgive and renew me. That, I think, is all the holiness any of us will reach on earth.

" . . . stop pretending that we have no problems . . . "

I am thinking of Mr Thomas again. He is a slimy character, but perhaps God has been working to change him. I don't know what he was like twenty years ago; it may be he had a long way to come. I can't compare his morality with someone else's. I can only hope that he is better than he would be without God at all.

Nor do I know what Mr Thomas is thinking inside. Maybe a sense of crisis is right now bringing him to the brink of change. I would not want to be the one who stepped in and condemned him the day before he gave in to God's urging.

But even if he never changes, what will that prove except that God wants us to be free? He wants an army of volunteers, not draftees. He will allow Mr Thomas – or me – to go on in hypocrisy. He allows each of us the dignity to make up his or her own mind. God's only force is the subtle, steady pressure of his Spirit on our minds.

God could force each of us today to come to terms with everything contradictory inside. If he did, I doubt many of us would have the strength to go on calling ourselves Christians. Instead, he brings our faults to us one at a time, and if we want to ignore them, we can. Since God allows freedom, there will always be hypocrites.

But when we do change our minds and let God's rule operate in our lives, he makes us free. We are free, most of all, to stop pretending that we have no problems. A hypocrite is someone hiding his or her problems inside, pretending they don't exist. A Christian is someone free enough to let his or her problems out and to give them each day to God.

T. S.

We've talked about hypocrites – people who act as if they are very religious but live in a way that contradicts the faith they claim. They make an obvious stumbling block for many young Christians.

Another kind of people, the legalists, may make just the opposite impression.

LEGALISM:
Why do 'good' Christians make me feel so far from God?

You are likely to be terrifically impressed by their rigorous faith. These super-dedicated Christians seem to know all the answers. And they make no compromises. They live strictly, and pour their lives into Christian concerns. They can inspire you.

Yet you may grow convinced, eventually, that they drive you away from God. Perhaps you will find that you simply can't live up to the rules that they insist on. Or perhaps you

*"They seem so
holy! So
sincere! So
dedicated!"*

will simply sense harshness underneath their
religiosity. You may feel in their attitudes
more than in their words that they have
grown proud, losing a sense of their dependence on Christ and his grace. Yet, if you are
typical, you will find it hard to put your
finger on what is wrong. They seem so holy!
So sincere! So dedicated! I, too, struggled for
years to understand whether there was
something wrong with these people's faith in
God – or whether the problem lay with me.

One strange character named Josh helped
me put it into perspective.

I met him at church: a strange, lonely guy.
Josh would seldom look you straight in the
face; he stared down, or sometimes over your
shoulder into the distance. He always looked
nervous, as if he were about to clear his
throat. Josh said little, and I had tried to
loosen him up by inviting him to the group.

The discussion that night was on what
makes a Christian unique. One man mentioned how Christians are the only ones who
have a reason for hope. The rest of the world,
he said, has to spend life depressed since
they couldn't be sure of an afterlife.

A woman talked about how Christians
have so much happiness and peace. Another, a young girl, mentioned that Christians have higher standards than others.

Josh sat silently through the discussion,
occasionally scraping his feet in imaginary
shapes on the floor. Later, when I asked him
about the evening, he didn't look up. He
said, 'Well, I always thought Christians were
people who admitted they were sinners. The
rest of us weren't supposed to have discov-
ered that yet. But tonight it seemed these

folks were proud of their religion. It's like they think they're superior to me or something.'

Josh's words cut deeply. I had sat smugly through the meeting, proud of my articulate friends with all the answers. But Josh helped me begin to see that I had forgotten about the word *grace*.

People who made Jesus angry

Jesus Christ knew various crooked people when he was on earth: sneaky tax-collectors, streetwalkers, thieves, ruthless soldiers. But as he travelled the streets of Jerusalem and other Jewish towns, one group particularly seemed to get under his skin. He singled them out for his strongest attacks. 'Snakes!' he called them. 'Tangle of vipers! Fools! Hypocrites! Blind guides! Whitewashed tombs!'

Strangely, the people who made Jesus livid with anger were the ones the American press might call 'Bible-Belt' fundamentalists today. This group, the Pharisees, devoted their lives to following God. They gave away an exact tithe, obeyed every minute law in the Old Testament, and sent out missionaries to gain new converts. There was almost no sexual sin or violent crime among the Pharisees. Weren't the Pharisees the type Jesus should have felt most comfortable with?

His reaction shows how seriously he viewed legalism. The Pharisees had the idea that we earn God's acceptance by following a list of definable, external rules. Legalism is especially dangerous because on the outside it looks so respectable. It creates clean-cut, pure, pious followers of God.

'' 'Tangle of vipers! Fools! Hypocrites!' ''

(*Matthew 23:13–27*)

*l*egalism today

I first ran into legalism in an extremely con-
servative church when growing up in
Atlanta, Georgia. It took only one month of
attendance to figure out what the list of
'don'ts' were in that church. The list included
dancing, cardplaying, smoking, drinking,
civil rights, movies, rock music, long hair,
games on Sunday, dice games, mini-skirts,
swimming with the other sex, and dating
blacks or Hispanics. If you stayed away from
all those 'evils' and carried a Bible you were
automatically accepted into the group.

Later in a Bible college in America's South,
I ran into a new list of rules. There, inte-
gration was supported but bowling, one of
the Atlanta church youth group's favourite
activities, was frowned on because some
bowling alleys served alcohol. Roller skating
was forbidden, because skaters had the habit
of holding hands while they skated and, besides, skating looked suspiciously like dancing.

The real hang-up at the Bible college
seemed to be with sex. So innocent an act as a
guy holding hands with a girl was banned.
Handholders or especially kissers who were
caught by a dean were quickly put on restric-
tion or dismissed from school. One teacher
went so far as to rail in class against lipstick,
which to him was a sign of harlotry.

Looking back, the Bible-college rules seem
sort of humorous. (They were enforced with
an iron fist and rarely seemed humorous at
the time.) The rules may have been exces-
sive, but were they actually harmful? They all
sound pretty innocent, hardly deserving of
strong words like those Jesus levelled at the

"It's as if you sign a contract . . ."

Pharisees. I would probably merely view them as a sort of joke, if it were not for the concern Jesus obviously had. What made him speak so strongly?

The Pharisees were dangerous, I believe, because they were so close to the truth. They believed in holiness, as God does, but they wanted the privilege of defining it. They snobbishly rejected any believers who did not follow their strict rules. They were so close to the truth that they could easily lead others astray – to confuse the truth with a close substitute. The Pharisees had a list of rules that you could follow to gain God's acceptance; God never had to give you a thing except his seal of approval. Jesus wanted people to find holiness as a gift from God.

In some ways the legalists I met were unlike the Pharisees. Few of them would have said that following their rules would earn God's acceptance. Yet they *acted* as if the rules were so important that God himself stood behind them. And they, too, tended to rate how 'spiritual' people were according to their rules.

*f*our subtle dangers

Almost every Christian group has its own form of legalism. The dangers are so subtle that Jesus focused on them, spelling out the problems with legalism in Luke 11 and Matthew 23. They can be summarized this way:

1. Legalism can be practised for show. When Pharisees prayed for long hours, they made sure they were out on a street corner to be noticed. They wore unusual clothing to call

" . . . and you're supposed to know all the fine print . . . "

" . . . a slip-up could get us expelled."

attention to how religious they were. The groups I was in never went so far as to require a specific uniform, as the Pharisees did, but I must admit the lipstickless, jewelleryless, skirt-dragging Bible-college girls were easy to spot. The danger here, Jesus warned, is that most outer looks could cover up a lot of hidden problems that need dealing with.

In my hall at Bible college there were guys who had severe problems with guilt over masturbation, anger with parents and authorities, racial discrimination, hatred of some political groups. Somehow those things stayed undercover most of the time. We paid more attention to the visible things; we had no choice – a slip-up could get us expelled.

Jesus' first warning was against the pride that legalism frequently produces. By obeying all the rules, the Pharisees began believing they really were morally superior to other people. At Bible college I noticed how students would rate other theological institutes: one college was 'liberal' because students could attend movies; another institute was tilting dangerously because it allowed such vices as holding hands as long as they were practised off campus. But we were still pure. We hadn't dropped our guard. We took a kind of perverse delight in being different.

2. It breeds hypocrisy. When rules are so clearly spelled out, it is easy to make the grade. Those who follow the rules soon relax in a sense of smug satisfaction, and it is easy to overlook hidden sins. Jesus said the Pharisees were like a cup that is clean on the outside and dirty on the inside. I could see the results of this in myself and my fellow students. We were too busy playing spiritual exercise games to show love and understanding to people who needed them. And we were too busy measuring skirt lengths to worry about war or racism or world hunger.

3. It is addictive. Legalism can be just as much a power game as climbing the corporate ladder, or climbing the social ladder in high school or college. In my school there was an unwritten game to see who could collect the longest list of school activities under his official photo. The winner was rewarded with status and a sense of power that he had beaten all the rest. Jesus said that even spirituality can be misused like that.

Christians can flex their muscles at each other as a technique for pumping up their own egos, while they gradually grow callous towards others. The vice-president of a company who clawed his way to the top is likely to have little sympathy for those still beneath him: 'I scrambled up the ladder; they can too.' When someone in our college committed a blatant sin, the natural response was to judge and ostracize rather than to forgive.

4. It lowers your view of God. Legalists fool you. They are so dedicated, so obviously concerned with their faith that you would think they have a very high view of God. But the danger in legalism is that it lowers the sights. If my requirements as a Christian are spelled out in a rulebook, that is *all* I have to do. The best legalists I knew felt secure and comfortable, like the Pharisees. They had fulfilled the law, had they not? But to those people Jesus shouts with a vengeance, 'Fools!' No-one ever *arrives* in the Christian life. We have to depend on God for the rest of our lives.

In summary, legalists miss the whole point

" . . . clean on the outside and dirty . . . inside."

of the gospel, that it is a gift freely given by God to people who don't deserve it. Legalists try to prove how much they deserve God's love. Assuredly, God is not impressed.

The rigid Old Testament law, Paul said, was like a schoolmaster to prove to us how far short of God we come. The law proves we cannot reach God, so God had to reach out to us, dying for us and restoring us to himself. Yet somehow legalists end up feeling more proud than grateful.

(Luke 11; Matthew 23)

After studying Jesus' extensive treatment of the Pharisees in the two chapters I have mentioned, I tried to trace a common thread. I believe that all these characteristics are natural results of people who associate only with each other all day. The Pharisees were simply around other Pharisees too much. They began competing with one another. By trying to impress each other with their love for God, they lost contact with the real enemy: Satan and his grip on non-Christians.

*n*ot an external exercise

Is legalism found only in America's 'Bible Belt'? No, legalism is like the common cold: no-one is exempt. It quickly spreads through any group. I know Christians who think themselves more spiritual and enlightened than others because they feel free to drink wine and smoke pipes. But they have the same legalist problems.

" . . . God is not impressed."

A meticulous researcher named Merton Strommen surveyed seven thousand American Protestant young people from many denominations, asking them whether they agreed with the following statements:

'The way to be accepted by God is to try sincerely to live a good life.' Over 60% agreed.

'God is satisfied if a person lives the best life he can.' Almost 70% agreed.

'The main emphasis of the gospel is on God's rules for right living.' Over half agreed.

It is as if the Apostle Paul and Martin Luther had never opened their mouths! Christians still seem to believe that following a code of rules gets you to heaven!

This kind of thinking can be fatal to a Christian's faith, and it may explain a troubling phenomenon among Christians. I have known dozens of kids who grew up in wonderful Christian homes and sound churches but decided later to scrap their faith. After being outstanding examples of Christianity for a while, they become spiritual dropouts.

" . . . out-standing examples . . . "

I have come to believe that many of them failed because they concentrated on the exterior, visible Christian life. When their Christian friends behaved a certain way and spoke a certain language, they began mimicking their behaviour. They became walking mirrors, reflecting all the correct styles and patterns of the church. Though there was no content to their faith, they were so skilled at following the rules that no-one noticed the inside. Faith as an external exercise is very easy to cast aside, as a snake sheds its skin. A person can discard a legalistic brand of Christianity just by trading it for a new set of rules, like those of Krishna Consciousness or Bahai or secular humanism.

If you develop Christian strength by focusing instead on the living Christ, it becomes much more difficult to shed.

" . . . become spiritual dropouts."

a word called grace

Jesus did not, of course, teach that holiness is unimportant. But he carefully avoided legalism. Several times people asked Jesus for advice on a specific problem. Usually he wouldn't give a specific interpretation of an Old Testament rule; instead, he pointed to the principle behind the rule. He didn't tell a rich person to give away 18.5% of his goods; he said give them all away. He didn't define adultery as actual sexual intercourse; instead, he condemned the principle of using women as sexual objects so that men commit adultery in their hearts. Love? That is not an easy thing to achieve even among friends. But Jesus says, 'Love your enemies!' Murder? 'I have added to that rule,' Jesus says, 'If you are merely angry, even in your own home, you are in danger of judgment!'

I could develop a list of very strict rules. But Jesus specialized in wiping out legalistic obligations by saying, 'No, there is much more to it than that.' He never replaces my goals with something easier. He replaces them with something impossible.

" . . . covered with his love."

Not that Jesus doesn't care about how we live. He does care, and that is why he continues pointing out the lofty principles which should guide our lives. Jesus lashes out at legalism so that we will never pile up a list of credits on how good we are. The credit goes to God, not to us.

Christians use a word called 'grace' that can be a cure for legalism. Grace simply means that God's love is freely given, with no strings attached. Grace is the opposite of legalism. Grace is what Jesus gave and gives.

Grace is the gift of Jesus himself.

the gospel explained

It is hard for me to accept gifts. I am used to achieving because I work at something. I get good grades or make the tennis team or sell an article only if I drive myself. So it is difficult for me to accept grace, too. I would rather *earn* God's favour. But because of grace, I don't have to go around trying to impress God with how spiritual I am. Grace helps me relax, to trust God, to realize he is already impressed enough to call me 'a gift that he delights in'. This is what Josh reminded me of so forcefully. Grace means that God is not finished with us yet – we are rough and unruly and cantankerous, but he still treats us as though we are the most beautiful of all his creations.

(*Ephesians 1:11, The Living Bible*)

Somehow Christians tend to forget about grace. We become *proud* of our faith because it solves some of our problems and sets us apart from other people. We forget that, as Josh said, the only consistent difference between us and the rest of the world is that we have admitted we are sinners. The only good in us is a result of God's free grace.

Paul said, 'Long ago, even before he made the world, God chose us to be his very own, through what Christ would do for us; he decided then to make us holy in his eyes, without a single fault – we who stand before him covered with his love.'

(*Ephesians 1:4, The Living Bible*)

P. Y.

O nce I watched a television interview with a famous Hollywood actress whose lover drowned in a harbour near Los Angeles.

CHAPTER

6

The police investigation revealed he had rolled off a yacht in a drunken stupor. The actress looked at the camera, her beautiful features contorted with grief.

SUFFERING:
Where is God when people are in pain?

She asked bizarrely, 'How could a loving God let this happen?'

The actress probably had not thought about God for months. But suddenly, in the face of pain, she lashed out in anger against him. For her and for nearly everyone, doubt follows pain like a reflex action. We hurt, and instinctively we turn against God regardless of the circumstances. We can't help blaming him and then doubting him.

In two decades of writing I have interviewed many people in pain. Some of them, like one teenage pilot who ran out of fuel and crashed in a cornfield, were directly responsible for their own suffering. Others, like a young woman who died of leukaemia six months after her wedding day, were seemingly struck at random with no warning. Yet all of them, without exception, experienced deep and nagging doubts about God because of the pain.

Pain calls our most basic beliefs about God into question. Over and over again I have heard four major questions brought on by pain: *Is God competent? Is he really so powerful? Is he fair? Why doesn't he seem to care about pain?* I know those questions well, for I have also asked them when I have suffered. If you have not yet asked them yourself, you probably will someday, when severe pain strikes.

"Is God . . . really so powerful?"

*i*s God competent?

When phrased that boldly, the question sounds strange and even heretical. But I believe many of our questions about pain trace back to the issue of God's competence. Does he know what he's doing? He created the whole world we live in. Couldn't he have done a slightly better job?

The world abounds with beauty, to be sure. Merely take a walk in a garden in the springtime, or watch snow fall on a mountain landscape, and for a moment all seems right with the world. Doubts vanish. The world reflects God's greatness as a painting reflects the genius of an artist.

But look closer at this lovely world and you begin to notice pain and suffering everywhere. Animals devour each other in a vicious food cycle. People destroy one another. And everything that lives eventually dies. God's 'painting' appears flawed, ruined.

I confess that I once viewed pain as God's one great goof in an otherwise impressive world. Why would he mess up such a world by including pain in it? Without pain and suffering, we would find it so much easier to respect and trust him. Why didn't he simply create all the beautiful things in the world, but leave out pain?

I lost my doubts about God's competence in a very unusual place. To my amazement I found that a world without pain actually exists within the walls of a leprosy hospital. As I walked the corridors of a leprosarium in Louisiana, USA, and got to know victims of the disease, my doubts faded away.

People with leprosy do not feel physical pain – that, in fact, is the peculiar tragedy of their disease. As the disease spreads, nerve endings that carry pain-signals fall silent. Thus, leprosy patients offer a window into what a painless world would look like.

Nobody I know envies the life of a leprosy victim. People normally respond to the disease with fear and revulsion. Why? Because of our visual images (often distorted through sensational novels and movies) of the disease. It is a cruel disease, and untreated it can cause gross deformity on the hands and feet and face. I know of no lonelier people in the world than leprosy victims.

But here is the most astounding fact about

"I lost my doubts . . . in a very unusual place."

leprosy, a fact that went undiscovered until the 1950s. Virtually all the physical deformity comes about *because the leprosy victim cannot feel pain*. The disease destroys only pain cells; all other tissue damage is caused by the patient's inability to sense pain.

I met a leprosy patient who lost all the toes on his right foot simply because he insisted on wearing tight and narrow shoes. I know another who nearly lost his thumb because of a sore that developed when he gripped a mop handle too hard. Scores of patients at that hospital have gone blind merely because leprosy silenced the pain cells designed to alert them when to blink. Over time, without blinking, their eyes dried out.

I learned that in a thousand ways, large and small, pain serves us each day. If we are healthy, pain cells alert us when to change shoes, when to loosen our grip on a mop handle or rake, when to blink. In short, pain allows us to lead a free and active life. If you ever doubt that, visit a leprosarium and observe for yourself a world without pain.

Without pain. My research into the nature of pain impressed me so much that eventually I wrote a book (*Where Is God When It Hurts?*) that describes some of the remarkable features of the pain network in our bodies. I cannot reproduce them all here, but a few are worth mentioning:

• Without pain's warnings, most sports would be far too risky.
• Without pain, there would be no sex, for sexual pleaure is mostly carried by pain cells.
• Without pain, art and culture would be very limited.

"Where is God when it hurts?"

• Musicians, dancers, painters, and sculptors all rely on the body's sensitivity to pain and pressure. A guitarist, for example, must be able to feel exactly where his finger lands on the string and how hard it presses.

• Without pain, our lives would be in constant mortal danger. Those rare people who feel no pain have no warning of a ruptured appendix, heart attack, or brain tumour. Most of them die young because of some medical problem that went undetected due to their insensitivity to pain.

I came away from my research into pain with a bedrock conviction that pain is essential to normal life on this planet. It is not an innovation God devised at the last moment of creation just to make our lives miserable. Nor is it his one great goof. That doubt has now vanished. I now look at the incredible network of millions of pain sensors all over our bodies, precisely gauged to our need for protection, and see an example of God's competence, not incompetence.

*I*s God powerful?

Of course physical pain is only the top layer of what we call suffering. Death, diseases, earthquakes, tornadoes – all of these summon up harder questions about God's involvement on earth. It is one thing to say he originally designed the pain system as an effective warning for us. But what about the world now?

Can God possibly be satisfied with all the rampant human evil and natural disasters and child-killing diseases? Why doesn't he step in with all his competence and put an end to some of the worst kinds of suffering? Is he powerful enough? Does he have the ability to rearrange the universe in a way that would relieve our suffering?

Not long ago a surprising book on this very topic edged up on the best-seller charts. It was a book about theology, by a rabbi, and it dealt with an unpleasant subject, the problem of pain. The book was called *When Bad Things Happen to Good People*, by Rabbi Harold Kushner.

Kushner's doubts about God began to surface when his infant son was diagnosed with the disease *progeria*. Somehow, no-one knows how, 'progeria' wildly speeds up the process of ageing. Instead of growing, a child with progeria starts shrinking just like a very old person. Kushner's son went bald. His skin turned leathery and wrinkled. Teeth that only recently had appeared started falling out. By the calendar the boy was barely school-age, but he had the body of an old man. Eventually, at the age of eight, he died.

During the agonizing progress of his son's disease, Harold Kushner still served as a rabbi. He had to go to widows and widowers, to people in hospitals, to other parents of suffering children, and represent God to them. He found that he could no longer believe some things about God.

A famous philosopher once posed the problem of pain this way: 'Either God is all-powerful or he is all-loving. He cannot be both and allow pain and suffering.' Ultimately, Kushner concluded that he too could no longer believe in an all-powerful, all-loving God.

" . . . 'progeria' wildly speeds up the process of ageing."

*"No apologies
from God."*

In his book, Kushner explains that he came to accept God's love, but began to question God's power. He now believes that God is good, and loves us, and hates to see us suffer. Unfortunately, God's hands are tied. He simply isn't powerful enough to straighten out the problems of this world – problems like children with the disease progeria.

Kushner's book became a best-seller because people found it comforting. They felt relieved. Kushner had voiced for them what they had wanted to believe all along: that God desired to help but could not. When we call on him to solve our problems, we are simply expecting too much of God.

I also found comfort in Rabbi Kushner's book – so much so that it began to trouble me. His ideas sound like something I may want to be true. But are they true? My problems grew larger as I studied the book in light of the Bible, a book given by God to tell us about himself and the nature of this world.

In one chapter, Kushner cites the book of Job, and I turned to the Old Testament book about a man who suffered great, undeserved pain. God delivered a speech to Job and his three friends after they had spent many long days thrashing over the problem of pain. If anyone deserved an answer to the problem of pain, it was Job. He, the most righteous man in the world, had suffered the most.

But the speech Job got (chapters 38 – 41) was not at all what he expected. No apologies from God. No 'Sorry, friend, but I had other things on my mind.' No real explanation of the problem of pain. Mainly, Job got a lesson in running the universe.

'Brace yourself like a man,' God began. 'I will question you, and you shall answer me.' Then God launched into a tour of the cosmos.

'Where were you when I laid the earth's
    foundation?
Tell me, if you understand.
Who marked off its dimensions?
Surely you know!'

(Job 38:4–5)

a matter of timing not power

Step by step, God led Job through the process of creation: designing the planet earth, carving out troughs for the sea, setting the solar system in motion, working out the crystalline structure of snowflakes. Then he turned to animals, pointing with pride to a mountain goat and the wild ox and ostrich and horse and hawk.

'Will the one who contends with the Almighty correct him?' God asked finally. 'Let him who accuses God answer him!'

(Job 40:2)

Novelist Frederich Buechner summed up the confrontation in Job this way: 'God doesn't explain. He explodes. He asks Job who he thinks he is anyway. He says that to try to explain the kind of things Job wants explained would be like trying to explain Einstein to a little-neck clam . . . God doesn't reveal his grand design. He reveals himself.'

With Job, God had a perfect platform to discuss his lack of power, if that indeed was the problem. Surely Job would have welcomed these words from God: 'Job, I'm truly sorry about what's happening. I hope you

"God doesn't explain. He explodes."

"I always thought my faith could get me through everything."

realize I had nothing to do with the way things turned out. I wish I could help, Job, but I really can't.'

God said no such thing. Speaking to a wounded, thoroughly demoralized man, he celebrated his own wisdom and power. If that is true – and you can read it for yourself in Job 38–41 – I must question Rabbi Kushner's theory about God's powerlessness. Why did God choose the worst possible situation, when his power was most called to question, to talk about his power?

Other parts of the Bible convince me that perhaps we ought to view the problem of pain as a matter of timing, not of power. We get plenty of indication that God is unsatisfied with the state of this world, surely as unsatisfied as we are. He doesn't like the violence, the warfare, the hatred, the suffering. And he plans to do something about it one day.

All through the prophets and through Jesus' life and the New Testament runs a theme of hope, of a great day when a new heaven and new earth will be fashioned to replace the old. The Apostle Paul puts it this way,

'I consider that our present sufferings are not worth comparing with the glory that will be revealed in us. The creation waits in eager expectation for the sons of God to be revealed. . . We know that the whole creation has been groaning as in the pains of childbirth right up to the present time.'

(Romans 8:18–19, 22)

At times, living in this 'groaning' creation, we cannot help feeling like poor old Job, who scratched his sores with shards of pottery and wondered why God was allowing him to suffer. Like Job, we are called to trust God, even when all the evidence seems stacked against him. We are asked to believe that he does control the universe and does have ultimate power, regardless of how things may appear.

And we must not make the mistake of judging God by the state of the world now. He plans a much better world someday, a world without pain or evil or tears or death. He asks for our trust in him and in his power to bring about that new creation.

*i*s God fair?

'Why me?' we ask almost instinctively when we face great tragedy. 'Two thousand cars were driving in the rain on the expressway – why did mine skid into a bridge?' 'Lift lines were crowded with skiers all day – why was I the one to break a leg and ruin my vacation?' 'A rare type of cancer strikes only one in hundred people – why did my father have to be among the victims?'

Look at those questions carefully and you can detect a common thread. Each questioner assumes that God was somehow responsible, that he directly caused the pain. If, in fact, he is all-competent and all-powerful, then doesn't that mean he controls every detail of life?

Did God hand-select which car would fishtail across the motorway? Did he direct one skier, but not others, to slalom over a hidden stump? Does he choose cancer victims at random out of a telephone book?

"He asks for our trust . . ."

63

Few of us can avoid such thoughts when pain hits us. Immediately we begin to search our consciences for some sin that God must be punishing: what is God trying to tell me through my pain? And if we find nothing definite, we begin to question God's fairness: Why am I suffering more than my neighbour, who is an outright jerk?

The suffering people I have interviewed torment themselves with such questions. As they writhe in bed, they wonder about God. Often, well-meaning Christians only make them feel worse. They come to the hospital room bearing gifts of guilt ('You must have done something to deserve this') and frustration ('You must not be praying hard enough').

"Does he choose cancer victims at random out of a telephone book?"

Once again, the only place to truly test out our doubts about God is the Bible. What do we find there – does God ever use pain as punishment? Yes, he does. The Bible records many examples, especially punishment directed against the Old Testament nation of Israel. But notice: in every case, punishment follows repeated warnings against the behaviour that merits the punishment. The books of the Old Testament prophets, hundreds of pages long, give a loud and eloquent warning to Israel to turn from sin before judgment.

Think of a parent who punishes a young child. It would do little good for that parent to sneak up at odd times during a day and whap the child without any explanation.. Such tactics would produce a neurotic, not an obedient, child. Effective punishment must be clearly related to behaviour.

The nation of Israel knew why they were

being punished; the prophets had warned them in excruciating detail. The Pharaoh of Egypt knew exactly why the ten plagues were unleashed against his land: God had predicted them and told him why they would happen and how a change of heart could prevent them.

Biblical examples of suffering-as-punishment, then, tend to fit a pattern. The pain comes after much warning, and no-one sits around afterwards asking 'Why?' They know very well why they are suffering.

But does that pattern resemble what happens to most of us today? Do we get a direct revelation from God warning us of a coming catastrophe? Does personal suffering come packaged with a clear explanation from God? If not, I have to question whether the pains most of us feel – a skiing accident, cancer in the family, a traffic mishap – really are punishments from God.

" . . . a skiing accident . . . a traffic mishap . . ."

Frankly, I believe that unless God specially reveals otherwise, we would be best to look to other biblical examples of people who suffered. And the Bible contains some stories of people who suffered but definitely were not being punished by God.

Once again, Job provides the very best example. He, too, questioned God's fairness, with good reason: God himself described Job as 'blameless and upright, a man who fears God and shuns evil'. Why, then, must he endure such an ordeal?

(Job 1:8)

Job's friends insisted the problem was with Job, not God. After all, they reasoned, God is fair and does not make mistakes. Job, despite his protests of innocence, must have done something to deserve his pain.

Why did Job suffer?

Thousands of years have passed, but we keep falling back on the same explanations of suffering that Job's friends voiced. We forget that those explanations were dismissed with a scowl by God at the end of the book. God insisted that Job had done nothing at all to deserve his pain. It was not a punishment for his behaviour.

Jesus made the same point in two different places in the New Testament. Once, his disciples pointed to a blind man and asked who had sinned to bring on such suffering – the blind man or his parents. Jesus replied that neither one had sinned. Another time, Jesus commented on two current events from his day: the collapse of a tower that killed eighteen people and a government-ordered slaughter of some worshippers in the temple. Those people, said Jesus, were no guiltier than anyone else. They too had done nothing to deserve their pain.

(John 9:1–5)

(Luke 13:1–5)

I have concluded that most Christians who suffer today are not being punished by God. Rather, their suffering fits the pattern of unexpected, unexplained pain such as that described by Job and the victims of the catastrophes Jesus described.

There are exceptions, of course. Some pain does have a clear connection to behaviour: victims of drunk driving and venereal disease don't need to waste time trying to figure out the 'message' of their pain. But for most of us, most of the time, I see no easy explanation for pain in the Bible.

" . . . no easy explanation . . ."

Why did Job suffer? Why did the man have to endure blindness? Why did those people get trapped in a falling tower? To such questions the Bible gives no neat answer. We live in an imperfect world, and not everything works out the way we wish. If anything, the book of Job implies that the answer is beyond human understanding. To figure out why everything in this world works the way it does is a bit like a little-neck clam trying to comprehend Einstein.

Consistently, the Bible directs the issue away from a question of cause to a question of response. 'Is God fair?' we ask in the midst of our pain. 'I am in control, no matter how it looks,' is his only answer. And then he has a question for us, one question: 'Do you trust me?'

"Is God fair?"

*d*oes God care?

The last great doubt that arises in the midst of pain is subtly different. Other questions are more abstract, philosophical. This one is personal. Why doesn't God show more concern for us in a time of need? If he cares about my pain, why doesn't he let me know it?

A great Christian author named C. S. Lewis wrote a classic book on pain called simply *The Problem of Pain*. In it he answered convincingly many of the doubts that spring up when Christians suffer. Hundreds of thousands of people have found comfort in Lewis's book.

But years after Lewis wrote the book, his wife contracted cancer. He watched her wither away in a hospital bed, and then watched her die. After her death, he wrote another book on pain, this one far more personal and emotional. And in that book, *A Grief Observed*, C. S. Lewis says this:

Meanwhile, where is God? This is one of the most disquieting symptoms. When you are happy, so happy that you have no sense of needing him, if you turn to him then with praise, you will be welcomed with open arms. But go to him when your need is desperate, when all other help is vain and what do you find? A door slammed in your face, and a sound of bolting and double bolting on the inside. After that, silence. You may as well turn away.

C. S. Lewis did not question the existence of God, but he did question God's love. At no time had God seemed more distant or unconcerned. Did God really love? If so, where was he at such a time of grief? Not everyone feels the sense of abandonment described by C. S. Lewis. Some Christians express that God became particularly real to them in their time of grief. He can offer a mysterious comfort that helps transcend the pain we are feeling. But not always. Sometimes he seems utterly silent. What then? Does God care only for people who somehow *feel* his comfort?

I have talked to enough people in pain to realize that experiences differ. I cannot generalize about how any individuals will experience the closeness or distance of God. But there are two expressions of God's concern that apply to all of us everywhere. One is the response of Jesus to pain. And the other involves everyone who calls himself or herself a Christian.

Even the most faithful Christians may, like

" . . . *prayers seem like words hurled into the void.*"

C. S. Lewis, question God's personal concern. At such a time, prayers seem like words hurled into the void. Few of us get a miraculous appearance of a loving God to calm our doubts. But at least we have this: an actual glimpse of how God truly feels about pain.

God did not sit idly by

In Jesus we have the historical fact of how God responded to pain on earth, and anyone who doubts God's love should take another look at him. He gives the up-close and personal side of God's response to human suffering. All our doubts about God and suffering should, in fact, be filtered through what we know about Jesus.

First there is the amazing fact that God himself took on pain. The same God who boasted to Job of his power in creating the world chose to subject himself to that world and all of its natural laws, including pain.

" . . . God himself took on pain."

Christian writer, Dorothy Sayers, put it this way:

For whatever reason God chose to make man as he is — limited and suffering and subject to sorrows and death — he had the honesty and courage to take his own medicine. Whatever game he is playing with his creation, he has kept his own rules and played fair. He can exact nothing from man that he has not exacted from himself. He has himself gone through the whole of human experience, from the trivial irritations of family life and the cramping restrictions of hard work and lack of money to the worst horrors of pain and humiliation, defeat, despair, and death. When he was a man, he played the man. He was born in poverty and died in disgrace and thought it well worthwhile.

(John 3:16)

'For God so loved the world,' says the Bible's most familiar verse, 'that he gave his one and only Son, that whoever believes in him shall not perish but have eternal life'. The fact that Jesus came and suffered and died does not remove pain from our lives. Nor does it guarantee that we will always feel comforted. But it does show that God did not sit idly by and watch us suffer alone. He joined us, and in his life on earth endured far more pain than most of us ever will. In doing so, he won a victory that will make possible a future world without pain.

"When Jesus' friend died, he wept."

The word 'compassion' comes from two Latin words that mean 'to suffer with'. Jesus showed compassion in the deepest sense when he voluntarily came to earth and took on pain. He suffered with us, and for us.

Jesus spent much of his life among suffering people, and his response to them also shows us how God feels about pain. When Jesus' friend died, he wept. Very often – and every time he was directly asked – he healed the pain.

How does God feel about our pain? Look at Jesus. He responded to hurting people with sadness and grief. And then he reached out with supernatural power and healed the causes of pain. I doubt that Jesus' disciples tormented themselves with questions like 'Does God care?' They had visible evidence of his concern every day. They simply looked at Jesus' face, and watched him as he performed God's mission on earth.

But Jesus did not stay on earth. Today we cannot fly to Jerusalem and book a personal appointment with him. What about those of us today? How can we sense God's love? We have the Holy Spirit, of course, an actual sign of God's presence in us. And we have the promise of the future when God will set the world right and meet us face to face. But what about right now? What can reassure us physically and visibly of God's love on earth?

That is where the church comes in, the community that includes every person on earth who truly follows God. The Bible uses the phrase 'the body of Christ', and that phrase expresses what we are to be about. We are called to represent what Christ is like, especially to those in pain.

The Apostle Paul must have had something like that process in mind when he wrote these words:

[God] comforts us in all our troubles, so that we can comfort those in any trouble with the comfort we ourselves have received from God. For just as the sufferings of Christ flow over into our lives, so also through Christ our comfort overflows.

(2 Corinthians 1:3–5)

There is only one good way to understand how the body of Christ can minister to a suffering person, and that is to see it in action. I have seen it, and I will end this chapter by telling you about Martha, a person who lived with great pain and great doubts.

Martha's story. Martha was a very attractive twenty-six-year-old woman when I first met her. Her life was permanently changed one

"Martha was a very attractive twenty-six-year-old woman . . . "

day when she learned she had contracted ALS, or Lou Gehrig's disease. ALS destroys nerve control. It first attacks voluntary movements, such as control over arms and legs, then hands and feet. It progresses on to involuntary movements, finally affecting breathing and causing death. Sometimes a person's body succumbs quickly, sometimes not.

Martha seemed perfectly normal when she first told me about her illness. But a month later she was using a wheelchair. She got fired from her job at an American university library. Within another month, Martha had lost the use of her right arm. Soon she lost the use of both arms and could barely move the hand controls on a new electric wheelchair.

I began visiting Martha at her rehabilitation hospital. I took her for short rides in her wheelchair and in my car. I learned about the indignity of her suffering. She needed help with every move: getting dressed, arranging her head on the pillow, cleaning her bedpan. When she cried, someone else had to wipe her tears and hold a tissue to her nose. Her body was in utter revolt against her will. It would not obey any of her commands.

We talked about death and briefly about the Christian faith.

I confess to you readily that the great Christian hopes of eternal life, ultimate healing, and resurrection sounded hollow, frail and thin as smoke when held up to someone like Martha. She wanted not angel wings, but an arm that did not flop to the side, a mouth that did not drool, and lungs that would not collapse on her. I confess that eternity, even a pain-free eternity, seemed to have a strange irrelevance to the suffering Martha felt.

She thought about God, of course, but she could hardly think of him with love. She held out against any deathbed conversion, insisting that, as she put it, she would only turn to God out of love and not out of fear. And how could she love a God who let her suffer so?

It became clear around October that ALS would complete its horrible cycle quickly in Martha. She had great difficulty in breathing. Because of reduced oxygen supply to her brain, she tended to fall asleep in the middle of conversations. Sometimes at night she would awake in a panic with a sensation like choking and be unable to call for help.

"I began visiting her at . . . hospital."

Martha badly wanted at least two weeks out of the hospital, in her own apartment in Chicago, as a time to invite friends over one by one in order to say good-bye and to come to terms with her death. But the two weeks in her apartment posed a problem. How could she get the round-the-clock care she needed? Some government aid could be found to keep her in a hospital room, but not at home, not with the intensive care she needed just to stay alive.

Only one group in all of Chicago offered the free and loving personal care that Martha needed: The Reba Place Fellowship of Evanston. That Christian community adopted Martha as a project and volunteered all that was necessary to fulfil her last wishes. Sixteen women rearranged their lives for her. They divided into work teams, traded off baby-sitting duties for their own children, and moved in. They stayed with Martha, listened to her raving and complaints, bathed her, helped her sit up, moved her, stayed up with her all night, prayed for her, and loved her. They were available. They gave her time and gave meaning to her suffering. To Martha they became God's body.

The Reba Place women also explained to Martha the Christian hope. And finally after seeing the love of God enfleshed in his body, the people around her – although to her God himself seemed uncompassionate, even cruel – Martha came to that God in Christ and presented herself in trust to the One who had died for her. She did not come to God in fear; she had found his love at last. On the faces of the women of Reba Place Fellowship she was able to read the love of God. In a very moving service in Evanston, she feebly gave a testimony and was baptized.

On the day before Thanksgiving day, 1983, Martha died. Her body, crumpled, misshapen, atrophied, was a pathetic imitation of its former beauty. When it finally stopped functioning, Martha left it.

But today Martha lives, in a new body, in wholeness and triumph. She lives because of the victory that Christ won and because of his body, the church, who made that victory known to her. She met God through her suffering, for it was during that time of suffering that she learned what he was truly like. In the love and compassion of the Christians around her, she saw the love and compassion of God himself. And her doubts about him gradually fell away.

"The Fellowship adopted her . . ."

P. Y.

74

i 've met some weird Christians . . . really weird, especially when I was younger. One guy named Samuel (he would

never let you call him Sam) was a fantastic tennis player. Because he thought tennis was a little unspiritual, you would have to coax him into playing a match.

THE INVISIBLE:
If 'seeing is believing', how can I maintain my faith?

On the court he was a demon (he would never let you call him that, either!): smashing backhands; looping high, precise lobs; demolishing the ball with an overhead slam.

Instead of swearing, Samuel reserved a nice Christian-sounding word to shout just before creaming the ball. About every fourth serve, his back would arch more steeply than usual, he would toss the ball higher, and his feet would leave the ground. Just before his arm whipped forward to whack the ball, he'd grunt loudly, ' 'Lujah!'

I still shudder when I think of that word ' 'Lujah'. Maybe Samuel meant it as an expression of his faith in God. But to me it was a final warning to dodge a missile which would come screaming over the net and up into my face. Though Samuel was pretty weird, he earned respect in almost any crowd by his inspired tennis playing.

Brian was the opposite – the butt of everyone's jokes. His 130 pounds were stretched along a 6'4" frame and, maybe because he didn't have enough strength to hold himself up, he walked with a permanent forward bend, as if he had carried a heavy backpack during all his growing years. Brian talked shyly and softly, and his face was so pale and fragile that you couldn't help mentally picturing him as a ghost.

To compound matters, Brian had the peculiar habit of walking around on his toes, backwards, memorizing Bible verses. That's the truth. Every night he would dress in a white sweatsuit, jog a loping mile, then cool off by walking in circles under a streetlight, *backwards*. It was an eerie scene: Brian's forward-tilting body jerking backwards along the perimeter of the streetlight's glow, his head bowed, straining to see the verse he'd printed on a card, mumbling to himself.

I admit, not all the Christians I knew were as weird as Samuel and Brian. But those two were given a special level of respect among Christians – as if their ' 'Lujah'-shouting and backward-walking-verse-memorizing elevated them to a special class. Among my young friends, most thought them more 'spiritual' than others. Knowing them, I kept asking myself, 'Is this what God wants?'

All the Christians, however, from Debbie, the blonde knockout, to George, the maths expert, shared the same traits which at first seemed every bit as weird as Samuel and Brian's eccentricities.

There was prayer, for example. The Christians I knew distorted events to make everything look like an answer to prayer. If an uncle sent them twenty-five pounds they would grin and shout and call a prayer meeting to thank God for it. While some people were sleeping off the night's activities, the super-Christians would sneak out of their homes at 6:30 a.m. to meet for a prayer session.

They seemed to take these 'answers to prayer' as final proof that a God was out there listening to them. I could always find some other explanation. 'Maybe that uncle sent *all* his nephews twenty-five pounds,' I would say. 'Some of the nephews aren't Christians. Was yours the only gift that answered a prayer?' They never discussed the frequent times God ignored their specific requests. Prayer, to me, was a foolish activity. Of what use was talking aloud to the walls?

*m*y phoney faith

But the super-Christians' earnestness dumbfounded me. Partly out of curiosity and partly out of a malicious desire to destroy their illusions, I started hanging around them, even acting 'Christian'. I made up

"I made up some story about how I got 'saved' . . . "

"Most of the girls were in tears."

some story about how I had been 'saved' as a teenager, embellished it with dramatic details, and told it at one of the Christian sharing meetings. The response was unbelievable. Most of the girls were in tears. Everyone hugged me, said 'Praise God!' and had a special prayer meeting of gratitude.

I began attending the prayer meetings – even the early morning eyeproppers – and imitated whatever the best Christians did. I learned the key to acceptance was a ritual called 'giving your testimony' in which your voice took on a soft, sincere tone and you told of some way the Lord had blessed you or 'spoken to you'. I found after a few weeks that I was one of the best testimony-givers of the bunch. I could often bring the group to prayers of thanksgiving, or beckon tears from their hungry, searching eyes.

Meanwhile, I would race back to my dorm after these sessions and tell my real friends how thoroughly I was hoodwinking all the Christians. In my mind, I had devastated their faith. I was a naturalist, and I believed there was no God. The only world existing was the world I lived in: rocks, trees and air. There were no 'spiritual beings'. Obviously their faith comprised spiritual jargon, a warm feeling of closeness, and a guilt trip all thrown together. Though an avowed unbeliever, I could pass for a veritable saint just by following the prescribed formula. Theirs was no different from any other misguided religion. How could God be real if all Christian experience could be duplicated by someone who did not believe in him?

*t*he plot thickens

A strange thing happened about a year after this experiment. It would have been humiliating and embarrassing had it not been so overwhelmingly delightful. I became a Christian. God met me in an amazing, undeniable way, at a time when I wasn't even looking for him – in fact, while I was hotly denying him. I experienced a true Christian conversion. During a routine (required) prayer meeting with friends, God made contact with me. He showed me his love and forgiveness, and I was born again.

Though I had spent my energy to that point trying to poke holes in the Christian faith and to sniff out inconsistencies in Christians, when God finally met me the change was so profound that I have never doubted it since.

How could I describe this experience to my sceptical friends whom I had succeeded in pushing towards agnosticism? How do you describe a world of colour to someone born colour-blind? I found myself mumbling the same imprecise phrases, like 'God completely transformed me' or 'God has changed my whole way of thinking, my sense of values' or 'He's given me peace I have never known before.' Most of my friends looked at me with an unknowing, confused, even *betrayed* look. I knew what they were thinking: 'It's finally gotten to the poor fellow. After months of hanging around those super-Christians, imitating them, he's cracked. He's loony.'

Frustrated, I tried to think of ways to persuade my friends that I had not gone loony, but rather had found a deeper reality. I knew

" . . . I had devastated their faith."

"The idea of miracles came to me."

they wouldn't be attracted to the Christians I knew – I had mocked them too successfully. The idea of miracles came to me. Could I find some absolutely unexplainable miracle? Surely that would prove God's reality.

*t*he need for proof

Why wasn't God more obvious? I wanted him to conduct well-orchestrated, televised miracles so that I could invite my sceptical friends to see an act of God they could never deny. The problem, as I saw it, was that the Christian acts – praying, loving each other, sharing faith with others, worshipping – just weren't *supernatural* enough to convince anyone that Christianity is true. *What we really need*, I thought, *is a giant, world-wide awesome display of God's power*. Naturalism would topple to the ground.

Even as I thought that, I realized it wouldn't work. The Bible records scores of instances when God really shocked the world. The ten plagues of Egypt, for example. Cecil B. DeMille spent millions to imitate them, and his film sequences still look phoney. What of the resurrection of Jesus? More than five hundred people attested that he had come back from the dead, but most people refused to believe them. God himself walked on earth for thirty-three years, teaching and performing astounding miracles. Yet, of those who heard him, only a minority believed.

Miracles – the wide-open, fireworks, supernatural sort – will always be an exception. Oh, I believe they occur. Many of my friends tell me of some miraculous healing, or a dramatic change God worked in a drug addict. But those miracles which suspend the laws of nature for an instant – I must admit I have never seen one personally.

I don't need miracles to believe; God has lovingly proved himself to me. It only bothers me when I think about my sceptical friends. If God really did a miracle, right in front of their eyes, would they believe? I don't know.

Instead I am left with the simple, sometimes tedious Christian acts of praying, sharing, loving, serving. As I know too well from my early contacts with weird Christians, those acts fall short of convincing a sceptic. They can even be expertly duplicated as a joke or as a sociology experiment.

I never did come up with a good strategy for convincing sceptics. Some came to believe, some didn't. Some were attracted to God by Christians' love; some fled to him when their world was crumbling. Many others, though, are far from God today.

*t*wo worlds

Today, even after all God has done for me, I have doubts. I will always believe he's real. But often my prayers seem like hollow, sleepy words that bounce off walls and rise no higher than my ceiling. Sometimes when I hear a fellow Christian describe an experience he or she has had with the Lord, it sounds no different from what you might hear at a Transcendental Meditation meeting or in an encounter group. It is still sometimes

"I don't need miracles to believe . . . "

hard for me to believe – *really* believe – that there is another part of the world out there. I am never completely rid of naturalism, because the only world I *see* everyday is the natural one. How do I keep believing in an invisible world?

There is an evident world around me comprised of trees and rocks and people and cars and buildings. Everyone believes in that one. But there is an equally real world of angels and spirits and God and heaven and hell. If only I could see that other world, just once, perhaps that would solve all my doubts.

When those doubts surface, I think back to some of Jesus' teaching about the two worlds. One incident especially pulled the two worlds together. Jesus sent out seventy of his faithful followers to the towns and villages he planned to visit later. He warned them sternly that they might be mocked or even persecuted for representing him. 'You are like lambs among wolves,' he said.

(*see Luke 10*)

The seventy disciples trudged away in the dust, certainly expecting the worst after Jesus' pessimistic warnings. But they returned exuberant. People had accepted them. Towns were eagerly awaiting the visit of Jesus. They had healed sick people. 'Even the demons submit to us in your name,' they breathlessly reported.

Jesus, who had been waiting for their return, gave a unique summary of what had happened. He said, 'I saw Satan fall like lightning from heaven!' Jesus brought the two worlds together. The world of the disciples had been one of walking over hot sand, preaching to mixed crowds, knocking on doors, asking to see the sick, announcing

"How do I keep on believing in an invisible world?"

the coming of Jesus. All their actions took place in the visible world which you can touch, smell, and see. But Jesus, with supernatural insight, saw that those actions in the visible world were having a phenomenal impact on the invisible world. While disciples were grinding out spiritual victories in the visible world, Satan was falling to their onslaught in the invisible world.

In Luke 12, Jesus gave some more clues to the effect that what happens here in the visible world affects the other world. He said that whatever we whisper in the inner rooms, thinking we are alone and safe, will one day be broadcast from the housetops for all to hear. No act, even whispering, is going unnoticed in the world. Each is recording its mark in the invisible world.

Both at the same time. Jesus said that when a sinner repents, the angels in heaven rejoice. Today you can watch a sinner repent. If you ever turn on a Billy Graham crusade being televised you can see, live and in colour, many sinners repenting. The camera zooms in on a middle-aged businessman, head lowered, threading his way down the stadium seats to talk to a counsellor. It moves to a young girl in Levis, quietly sobbing in a corner as a friend explains the Bible to her. According to what Jesus said, while those visible acts are taking place, some tremendous invisible acts are also occurring. The angels are throwing a celebration in heaven. The two worlds are working as one.

The Man Jesus was, of course, the ultimate example of the two worlds working as one. He was a man with sweat glands, hair, fingernails, and all the characteristics which define humans. Yet inside that body God lived.

All of us who are Christians believe in the invisible world; we merely forget about it. We get consumed by our world of arguments, relationships, jobs, and school – even the 'religious' world of church and prayer meetings. Perhaps if Jesus were standing in the flesh beside us murmuring phrases like 'I saw Satan fall' whenever God used us for some good, we would remember better.

The world we live in is not an 'either/or' world. The actions I do as a Christian – praying, worshipping, loving – are not exclusively supernatural or natural. They are both, working at the same time.

"The world . . . is not an 'either/or' . . . "

Seeing the invisible

As reminders of the supernatural world we are given God's Spirit, who permanently dwells within us. We are given the good counsel of the Bible and of fellow Christians, who affirm with us that, yes, there is another world, and God is alive and cares about us.

Besides all these specifically Christian reminders, there are many proofs of God in the world which can be detected by everyone. Do you wish to see an expression of God's power? Get up early to watch a sunrise. Visit California's beaches during whale migration season and watch the great beasts frolic and sputter.

Do you question whether man is immortal? Consider your own reaction when you pass a dead cat or rabbit on the road. You may feel a twinge of regret or sadness, especially if you love animals; but it is not at all the reaction you would feel if you passed a human body sprawled next to the pavement. You would gasp and screech to a halt. The memory would burn into your mind. You would never forget the scene. What is the difference? Both corpses are made of sinew, blood, bone, and organs. The difference is nothing visible; it is the fact that the person is immortal, made in God's image.

Sometimes I remember the invisible world clearly. I can sense its existence so strongly that it seems more real than the visible world. The quality of *faith* lets me believe – the quality that the Book of Hebrews defines as 'being sure of what we hope for and certain of what we do not see'. At those moments (I remember how I felt after my conversion) I wonder how anyone could doubt. Other times – often when I'm tired and irritable, and have just fought with someone – I can barely remember the invisible world. Those moments, too, are evidence of the great spiritual struggle going on behind the curtain, accompanying every moment of my life.

(Hebrews 11:1)

'There is no neutral ground in the universe,' said C. S. Lewis. 'Every inch, every split second, is claimed by God and counter-claimed by Satan.'

I am strong enough to believe that on my own sometimes. I feel very much a part of a battle. But at other times I forget and must be pressed back to God, to his Word, to the helpless dependence on him and his followers here on earth. They remind me of the invisible world and my role in it. Satan does not give up his ground easily.

"I feel . . . part of a battle."

P. Y.

my doubts about God come most often in crowds. I stand still and watch streams of people flow by me. Each

C H A P T E R

person intent on his or her own direction and his or her own thoughts. Each, I think, knows and cares nothing about my belief that there is a God who cares.

STRATEGY FOR DOUBTERS:
What do I do with my unanswered questions?

I feel lonely and insignificant, numbed by the democracy of unbelief. Who am I to say that my reasoning makes more sense than theirs? They look so solid and sure in their business: how could I ever convince them of a God who loves them? They aren't even interested. I wonder if it is I who am crazy.

Does it make you uncomfortable to know that I, who should be a sturdy, reliable believer, have doubts? That there have been nights when I literally screamed at God, pleading for some signal that he is real? There was a time when I felt threatened if a Christian told me of his own deep questions. If others thought of deserting the ship, was I only kidding myself to keep on believing? Besides, I thought doubts were the worst danger to a Christian.

I do not think so now. Doubts are serious. Sometimes they lead to a rejection of God. But more often, I think, if confronted honestly, they can lead to a stronger faith.

Other things worry me more.

It worries me when someone is knowingly disobeying God and rationalizing away his disobedience. Nothing destroys faith sooner.

It worries me when someone pastes on a facade of vibrant faith, while doubts and loneliness lurk behind.

It worries me when someone is finding a 'new, more mature' faith that finds unnecessary such things as knowing the Bible, praying, and worshipping with other Christians.

But doubts? They have their place, in the Bible at least. From the flaming questions of Job to the puzzled, stubborn 'Show me' of Thomas, doubts are handled frankly. Doubters are brave enough to ask questions; in fact, it is the pious people who seem to anger God more by knowing all the answers and quickly shutting-up questioners.

When you are doubting God's existence, it may help to figure out just what is in doubt. Analyse your problem before you look for a solution. But do seek answers. The walls of Christian faith are not so thin that you will break holes in them by pushing too hard. If you ask honestly, you will find answers –

" . . . numbed by the democracy of unbelief."

though not always the answers you would have liked. 'Seek and you shall find,' Jesus promised. 'Knock and it shall be opened to you.' That was a promise to his disciples. They had chosen to follow him. Having done so, they heard the promise from Jesus himself, who founded the earth, that they would not remain puzzled for ever, so long as they were willing to seek and ask.

(Matthew 7:7)

three kinds of doubt

Lonely doubts, I think, are the most common. I talked recently with a friend who had been going through a difficult time doubting whether God exists or cares at all. But recently her thinking changed. 'I realized,' she said, 'that I was really lonely. I knew all these people, but none of them really knew me. So I was angry with God, yelling at him that I didn't have any friends. That was the real source of my doubts.'

It is hard to believe in God's love when there are no people around who love you. It takes unusual strength to live through such a period without severe doubts. We are meant to experience God's love through people, as well as through God himself.

But if you are lonely, make sure that is the focus of your doubts. Do not go on a philosophical tangent about those suffering in India. Speak to God about the reality of human friendship, and ask him to begin to show you how to make one good friend. Ask him, too, to show some purpose in your loneliness, some way you should grow through it. It won't happen overnight, but

"If you ask honestly, you will find answers . . ."

with a sense of direction your doubts about God will fade. He will become your ally, not your antagonist, in healing loneliness.

*"Speak to God
. . ."*

Crisis doubts are often the most intense. Someone you love dies. Perhaps your best friend rejects you. Exams destroy you. Often, during a crisis, you are very tired without even knowing it. The mental strain makes you need far more rest, and you often get no physical exercise. You're nervous.

In *God and Man at Yale*, William F. Buckley said that whenever he had doubts about God he would lie down until he got over them. It is not so bad a prescription. Often doubts, and particularly crisis doubts, are a response to powerful feelings of sadness fuelled by fatigue. They will pass. Of course, crises can and should start questions that have lasting implications. But don't delude youself by thinking that you can settle the meaning of the universe in one evening when you are low on sleep. You are not in any shape to do that. Recognize that you are in a crisis, ask your questions, but store them until later. Sleep if you can. Look to a friend for comfort. Often all it takes is a chance to express your doubts, and they fly away. If not, don't make any great decisions. Wait to resolve your questions later when you are rested.

Intellectual doubts are actually, I believe, least common of all. The reason is that very few of us are intellectuals. But many of us wish we were, and it is hard for us to admit that we cannot figure out all the answers for ourselves. So we phrase many of our doubts as intellectual questions, partly to keep at a distance our own loneliness and inadequacy.

There are, however, really good questions to be asked about the reality of Jesus Christ. If God is good, why is he willing to send some people to hell? How can we say that Christianity is better than Hinduism? Why do people suffer? If offering our lives to God really makes us new creatures, how come Christians often seem no better than anyone else? How can we trust in a book as unscientific as the Bible? There are many more.

I am not going to try to answer those questions here, though I believe there are good answers. We may not find final, once-for-all answers to questions. But we will find answers that have satisfied men and women a great deal smarter and more learned than we. (A good starting place might be the writings of C. S. Lewis, particularly *Mere Christianity* and *The Problem of Pain*.)

" . . . very few of us are intellectuals."

The saddest thing to me is that those who ask intellectual questions often decide the answers – and their whole life – on the basis of a few vague ideas floating around in their heads, or something a professor in college said with assurance, or on information in a couple of short-cut textbooks. There is better information in any library or bookstore and, I would hope, in any pastor's office.

If you are having intellectual doubts, follow them honestly to the end. Ask questions of people who are likely to have answers, and ask a number of people – don't settle for one or two. Ask for reading material. It may take some time, but since you are trying to decide whether your life as a Christian has meaning, isn't the question worth some serious study?

If it is not – if you are content with the rummage sale of information in your brain already – then I doubt whether you are really being honest in your questions. If you give up your faith, you have cheated yourself. If you maintain your faith, you have cheated yourself too: these questions may come up again, or your faith may become superficial if you are afraid to confront difficult doubts and listen to questions non-Christians are asking.

If you ask honestly and are willing to ask God for help, I think you will find answers that satisfy. That is what has happened to me time and time again.

"Ask questions . . ."

*t*he ultimate answer

My doubt is more emotional than intellectual; I know that because it comes when I am tired. Still, it is real. I get weary of being different. Sometimes I would like to drop back into thinking what everyone else thinks. Instead of worrying about other people, instead of reading the Bible and praying and going to church, I would like just to think and do what *I* feel like. Being a Christian seems to be a tiresome ritual I'm caught in.

So what happens when I have these doubts? One thing that needs to happen, of course, is sleep. But there is more than that. My questions are not bad ones. What *is* the point of all these rituals we go through? Why *do* Christians act and think in such an odd way? I am forced back to the foundation of my faith. It comes down to this: if it were not for Jesus, I don't think I would be a Christian.

Now, isn't that an absurd sentence? If it

"Now isn't that . . . absurd?"

weren't for Jesus, there would be *no* Christians. There would be no Christianity. But, obvious as the point is, it needs to be made. Sometimes I think our version of Christianity could cruise along without Jesus. If someone somehow proved Jesus never lived or never came back to life, we might get along just as well. We get rosy feelings from singing songs together. We make good friends through church or Christian groups. We have a point of view for looking at the world, and that breeds security. We talk about Jesus, but that seems to be a coded language for our good feelings. It doesn't attach to any real person – a person as definite as, say, my father. Could we substitute any other name for 'Jesus' and, once we got comfortable with it, do just as well? Would 'Buddha' do?

Suppose that we were to live Christianity just that way – strictly as a way of life, without really thinking of it as a relationship with Jesus, a real, living person. I suspect that we might keep to the pattern all our lives enjoying being a Christian in the same way people enjoy being Labour activists. Over the years we would grow to understand the system better – we would know how to argue over crucial points, where to find things in the Bible, and have theories about how a church should run. But we would probably not grow kinder or more compassionate or closer to the source of life. We might spend the whole of our lives confusing the good feelings we get from praying in a group of friends with the reality of God. We might never know we had missed anything.

I think most people start with Christianity and only gradually grow to know Christ. We are attracted by a group of people, a way of life, a leader or friend we trust.

That is my experience. I grew up in a fine Christian family. I have known some wonderful Christian leaders. I have been in some great churches, some exciting fellowships where things were really happening. But as good as all that is, it is not enough. You have to go beyond. Though some of the Christianity I have been around has been very good, long dry spells still came when my faith didn't mean much to me, or when I was without much support from other Christians.

But what I cannot get around is the man known as Jesus. He is amazing. The more I learn about him, the more astonished I become. He is the ultimate answer to my doubts.

*t*he only truly free man

You have to read about him. In fact, there isn't any other completely reliable way to learn about him. Four pamphlets give reasonably detailed accounts of his life on earth, when his character took on a visible focus. It is no accident that the New Testament begins with them: Matthew, Mark, Luke and John. They are basic.

What do I find in these four accounts of Jesus? I find layer after layer of meaning; simplicity I can understand the first time I read it; and richness the greatest of minds never exhausts. I find a convincing portrait of the only man I would think it is worth dying to follow.

It is not just what he said. It is not just his ability to do amazing things. It is not just the way he loved people. It is not just his

"Would 'Buddha' do?"

"Even death could not take away who he was . . ."

character under stress. It is not just his astonishing relationship with God. Incredibly, he combined all those things. He is unique; there is nothing and no-one like him.

I could talk about many aspects of Jesus and why he appeals to me. But I will limit myself to telling you just one thing that always amazes me. Jesus is the only completely free man I have ever encountered.

I want so much to be free. I don't want to be imprisoned by anything. I want to soar as wildly as a hawk in the wind. In Jesus I see a model for what I want to become.

By 'free' I do not mean free from all constriction or responsibility. People who have that kind of freedom are often tragically enslaved. Rock stars, with all the money and time to do what they like, sometimes commit suicide or strangle slowly on drugs. Some of the freest people seem to be those under intense pressure, like Aleksander Solzhenitsyn or the Apostle Paul in prison.

The freedom I am interested in starts inside. I figure we will always have some limits imposed from the outside. I am more concerned about the limits we have inside. A really free person is able to laugh when others are bitter; he can be kind when others hate; he can be in a room full of gossip and not participate; he can be himself no matter what pressures are on him.

Jesus was free. Crowds adored him, but he did not live to please them. Hundreds of sick people came to him to be healed, but he did not let that pressure keep him from priorities like spending time in prayer. The religious establishment criticized him, but he did not let that intimidate him, nor did he let it push him into becoming a stereotyped rebel. His best friends had ideas about how he should act and the kind of future he should expect, but he would not be influenced.

Jesus' freedom flowed from his identity as God's Son. He kept in contact; he remembered who he was in relation to God. The pressures could not mould him, because God did not change in his love and his promise to keep him together. Even death could not take away who he was – and is.

For me, his most amazing display of freedom was in front of a rigged court that was obviously bent on murdering him. These were the religious people; they were also everything he had stood against. Now, in the ultimate display of perverted piousness, they had him in their power. They didn't even have the courage to kill him outright: they had to try him on phoney charges.

" . . . and is."

*f*rom doubt to freedom

If you can imagine being accused of bribery in front of the Supreme Court by the best-known cheat in politics, you might have a hint of the mix of fury and fear natural to anyone in that situation.

Most of us have enough guilt stored up to feel we deserve punishment of some kind. When my car breaks down, I glumly, fatalistically accept it as something I deserve. But Jesus had done *nothing* wrong, not one thing in his whole life. He had never felt guilt.

So wouldn't you expect Jesus angrily to defend himself? Or to try to talk his way out of death? Or to beg?

He did not. At his trial he was repeatedly asked if he believed himself to be the Messiah, the Son of God. He was challenged to defend himself. He never did.

Why? In Luke 22:67–68 Jesus says why: 'If I tell you, you will not believe me, and if I asked you, you would not answer.' Even under threat of a grossly unfair, torturous death, Jesus remembered who he was. He knew they had the roles reversed: he was the judge of the world, and they were the ones who needed to defend themselves. They could play at mock trials, but he wasn't going to be caught in their game.

That was not arrogance. It was reality. The unreality was the trial, which tried to over-rule the position God had given Jesus. He went to his death a perfectly free man. Even on the cross, in horrible pain, he was himself. What did he do in those last, agonizing hours while he felt his body dying? He forgave a thief. He initiated a family relationship between his mother and John. He committed his life to God.

I can't get over that. When I read what happened I am astonished. I know that I have found contact with someone worth following. I conquer my doubts. Not only that, I give thanks for my doubts, for they have led me closer to Jesus himself.

Your doubts can often lead to a deeper understanding of God, for his answers will seldom be just the kind you were expecting. If your beliefs are shallow, then they will have to be dredged deeper. If the skeleton of your faith has grown crooked, bones may have to be broken before they can be reset. It will hurt. But don't be afraid: broken bones set stronger.

"It will hurt."

T. S.